CIPHER
in the
CROPS

The Fractal and Geometric Circles of 1991

EDITED BY BETH DAVIS

GATEWAY BOOKS, BATH

First published in 1992
by GATEWAY BOOKS
The Hollies, Wellow,
Bath, BA2 8QJ, UK

© Gateway Books 1992

Distributed in the USA
by Atrium Publishers
11270 Clayton Creek Rd
Lower Lake, CA 95457

Cover design — Studio B of Bristol
Front cover photo — David Parker/Sci. Photo Lib.
Back cover photo — Calyx Photo Serv.

Set in Sabon 10½pt on 12½ by
Ann Buchan Typesetters
of Shepperton, Middlesex

Text printed and bound by
The Cromwell Press
Broughton Gifford, Wilts.

Colour section by
Tabro Litho of Huntingdon

British Library Cataloguing-in-Publication Data
A catalogue record for this book, is
available from the British Library

ISBN 0-946551-93-6

Contents

Foreword

Beth Davis

In 1990 a group was formed to collectively study the crop circle phenomenon. It was to bring together most of the acknowledged experts in the field. The first meeting was held at my home, a small farmhouse in Cambridgeshire. The excitement of new beginnings was tempered by the practical problems of organisation, and the over-riding view that the study group was to provide an open forum for debate, where the crop circle phenomenon could be shared openly with a wider public.

The Centre for Crop Circle Studies in now a firmly established organisation disseminating information to a world-wide membership. To its credit are two publications from Gateway Books, *The Crop Circle Enigma*, edited by Ralph Noyes, 1990,[1] and *Crop Circles: Harbingers of World Change*, edited by Alick Bartholomew, 1991.[2] The first of a CCCS monograph series, *Crop Circle Classification*, by Patrick Palgrave-Moore,[3] also emerged in 1991.

Because of the transitory nature of the crop circle formations, capturing their beauty of form and detail in the fields is of paramount importance. There are archives of photographs and drawings held by individuals who have pioneered the recording of the phenomenon, and, more recently, collected by newer researchers. The task of collating this information will be Herculean.

The question of whether the crop circle formations were hoaxes or not has exercised many minds, particularly during and since the 1991 season. Hoaxing almost became a cult practice! It seemed that some hoaxed crop circles were formed out of curiosity and experiment, others by a need to defuse a potentially 'frightening and evil' situation, while some were beaten out by jokers for the fun of it, and possibly others were formed for reasons accountable only to the peculiar nature of the human psyche — to be counter-productive, to damage or to find ways of control. Despite all these possibilities, hoaxing cannot account for more than a fraction of the enormous number and variety of formations that there have been. There have, of course, been many more claims than actual man-made circles!

The compound formations still bear the hallmark of the earlier simple circles in the way the corn is laid, but their cause is enigmatic and their details are being studied scientifically to give us data about their phenomenal qualities. The first results from analysis of stems and seed-heads of affected crops were published in 1991: *Scientific Evidence for the Crop Circle Phenomena*, by Montague Keen[4] who has also edited a *Field guide*, to help standardise surveys of the circle formations.

At the climax of the 1991 season there were three unique formations, two in Wiltshire, and one in Cambridgeshire, each spectacular for its size and quality of design and execution. It seems appropriate now to make a permanent record of these outstanding occurrences before their memory is erased by time. The contributors to this account experienced these formations at first hand; the formations' meaning is tentatively explored here in this book.

Easton, Cambridgeshire

NOTES

1. *The Crop Circle Enigma*, ed. Ralph Noyes, Gateway Books, 1990.
2. *Crop Circles — Harbingers of World Change*, ed. Alick Bartholomew, Gateway Books, 1991.
3. *Crop Circle Classification*, Patrick Palgrave-Moore, CCCS, 1991.
4. *Scientific Evidence for the Crop Circle Phenomena*, Montague Keen, CCCS, 1991.
5. *Field Guide*, Centre for Crop Circle Studies publication, 1992.

ACKNOWLEDGEMENTS

I would like to thank all the cereologists who in one way or another have contributed to this book by sharing information, photographs and drawings with the authors. Credit also goes to their families and friends who must have so patiently endured their concentric obsession! I would especially like to thank Alick Bartholomew as co-editor and publisher, for his inspiration in this venture.

Introduction

Beth Davis

"Science is like a crossword puzzle: nature presents the clues, and they hang together in an intelligible order, with an underlying pattern and design . . ."

Paul Davies, author of *Superforce*, radio interview with Brian Magee, 1991.

The phenomenon of our age, the appearance of the crop circles in the cornfields of England, could be viewed as a vital clue to a cosmic crossword. The clues are a developing language, on whose meaning we can only speculate. The physical origins of crop circles are as yet unknown; they are often associated with earth-light phenomena, their effects are sometimes felt, and they can clearly be seen. They are certainly no accident of nature: they were intended to take the form they have, and their siting would also seem to have been predetermined.

They are not signs giving directional information, but symbols of meaning, of our time and time past. It is perhaps the *unprecedented* nature of these events that has excluded them from scientific analysis so far. In the ancient and classical worlds, both science and mathematics were sacred. Mathematics held the key to the secrets of nature, as the language of the natural world. Science became the intellectual response where theories were tested, and the accepted results became the building blocks of man's understanding of himself and the world around him — answers to some of the clues.

The first crop circle impressions were not widely recognised. There are several reports from farmers of crop circles recurring on their land over a period of twenty years or more. Simple circles silently appearing at dawn, with diameters up to twenty metres, and a clockwise lay of corn — these were the common themes. The simple form of circle was noted particularly in the Wiltshire area of south England in the late 1970's. By the turn of the decade it had aroused the interest of a number of people recording the light-effects of the UFO phenomena.

The number of circles recorded in 1980 could be counted in hundreds; by 1989 the number had increased to thousands. The simple circle had now developed to a *formation*, with several elements or parts. The circles were laid spirally, concentrically clockwise or counter-clockwise, and radially, as though purposefully to confound the theories of a natural source for their construction. Bands, segmental patterns, rings, and small satellite circles distributed symmetrically, were part of the composition. Their beauty was remarkable. The formations occasionally had natural additions made to them on subsequent days.

Records in the late 1980s were received from other parts of Britain, other countries in Europe and across the world. This was a pandemic phenomenon. Meanwhile in 1990, the formations were compounded by other additions to the circle form: they became linear in style, they were connected by pathways, had segments or rings at their heads, developed tails, fins, keys or simple rectangular boxes, or detached circles. In 1991, signatures to the Wiltshire formations identified them with certain types. Were these genuine or a man-made hoax? In Cambridgeshire and elsewhere the construction of the formations clearly identified each one by a *family code*. Comparisons of photographs show these characteristics in the lay of the corn, and in their design and form. Where circles have been repeated from one season to the next in the same field, they show common lay features.

The developing circle formations could appear to be a form of communication by the use of symbols. Ancient mystical symbols have been identified by archaeologists and laymen alike; they relate to the cosmos and the spiritual qualities of our being. Are these clues of a crossword? Three formations of 1991 were outstanding. They were symbols that were clearly recognisable today. Exquisitely engraved in the corn, one is a symbol of sacred geometry, one is from the language of modern mathematics and a model for the natural world; and yet another could be a section of the human chromosome, bearing the genetic code for our existence.

We await future sets of clues, uncertain that we have solved those clues we have been given already.

THE LABYRINTH.   The Mandelbrot formation holds within the cardioid
the form of a labyrinth, which since primordial times was a symbol of the
journey of the soul. At birth a human enters the labyrinth and follows a path
of spiritual enlightenment. The path folds back on itself in a clearly described
way, known as the 'Great Turning' and the 'Little Turning', which are points
of initiation on the way to fulfilment. The centre of the labyrinth is the final
goal where the soul achieves the light of full knowledge and is reborn.
The spiralling circle with the two distinct lobes of the path-turnings on
ancient tombs may have described death and the re-entry to the womb of the
earth, where the spirit is reborn. The labyrinth form may also be a symbol of
the cosmic dance, the whorling of planets and atoms in the creation of matter
from chaos, around a pivotal force – the Divine Light.

The Ickleton Mandelbrot Formation

Beth Davis

"God has put a secret art into the forces of Nature so as to enable it to fashion itself out of chaos into a perfect world system"   Immanuel Kant.

This most beautiful formation was the first ever to have a recognisable contemporary form. It was found on August 12th 1991, near the village of Ickleton, in Cambridgeshire, and ten miles south of the university city of Cambridge. Just two fields away is the ancient trackway of the Icknield Way. The formation was almost precisely aligned to a simple clockwise circle that had appeared in June, in the parish of Fowlmere to the north-west.

The neighbouring farmers had been harvesting their fields that week, and were unaware of the formation until the news was broken on Tuesday. Mr Hugh Raybone, on whose farm it had occurred, said he hadn't a clue what had caused it. Chris Bates, a farmer and former helicopter pilot, flew over the formation with a friend, taking a cinefilm that was later to be used by John McNish in his video film of the season, *Crop Circle Communique*[1]. His view was that it could not have been made by any conventional farming machinery.

The heart shape (cardioid) had two pendant circles, and perimeter circles arranged like jewels. Between the larger circles on the perimeter of the cardioid and the first pendant circle were tiny circles that could barely be seen from the air. A small circle was connected by a tractor tram-line impression to the formation below the pendant circles. The formation was precise in its execution, and almost perfect in its axial symmetry, which was subtly expanded to the eastern side.

Dick and Mary Wombwell, who farm the nearby fields, visited the formation several times with their family. Dick told me later how overwhelmed he had been when he first walked into the formation. "The corn was laid down in a clockwise manner, each stem was bent over at the same height above the ground, about half an inch, the stems were not crushed, and the ears of corn were intact. The seed was still in the husk even though the crop was about ten days from harvesting." Mary Wombwell and her daughter-in-law noticed the single stems of standing wheat between the circle formations. "No one could have made this in the dark, and if there were any lights to aid them we would have noticed them from the farmhouse."

Earth-lights are occasionally recorded in the Cambridge area. On August 11th 1991, Mrs Urwin was driving home with her son along the B1102 towards Swaffham Bulbeck. It was 1.15am. She noticed a silver blue ball of light travelling at the same speed as the car, and approximately 30feet from it. The light followed the car for about 10 seconds and then suddenly disappeared when it appeared to converge with the car. The previous night at Great Wilbraham a similar light had been seen. This was the day before the Mandelbrot was formed and these events were reported in the *Cambridge Evening News*[2].

A Cambridge Controversy

The news did not break in Cambridge until Thursday 15th August, in the local press. A photographer from a national paper, *The Daily Mail*, had taken photographs at the invitation of Mr Cherry-Downes to fly with him, but the paper had not printed them. The local paper, however, did[3]. It was first described as heart-shaped, but was quickly recognised in Cambridge to be a representation of a *Mandelbrot Set* of fractal geometry. This cipher could not have been more appropriate for Cambridge.

A Mandelbrot Set is a most intriguing and beautiful formation of infinite dimension, created mathematically on the computer. The Ickleton formation was not a perfect representation, and the design was also without 'solar flares'. "Solar flares on the computer-produced design cannot be eliminated from the formula unless the design is artificially trimmed", was the reported comment of Dr David Battison, a computer scientist in Cambridge.

Regarded as the most complicated object in mathematics, the Mandelbrot Set was discovered by Dr Benoit Mandelbrot when he began to use high-powered computers to draw these *fractals* in the 1960's described by George Wingfield (see *Chaos*, by James Gleick[4]). When Dr Benoit Mandelbrot was told of the formation, he said he was very pleased to hear of the theory taking root . . . "It's certainly pleasing to be remembered in this way. But I can tell you, I plead not guilty. Was it a student joke? I don't think it is the work of extra-terrestrials, I can't wait to see what the next one will look like." So reported the *Sunday Telegraph*, 25th August 1991.

The debate was opened; it could *only* be a hoax! Letters filled the pages of the Cambridge papers, and rumours abounded: "It was the work of engineering students? The mathematics department? A maths student!" — clearly heard at a college high table one evening. Yes, surely this was the answer. This information was conveyed to Montague Keen, an agronomist and research member of the Centre for Crop Circle Studies. More rumours circulated after the summer recess when the students returned to Cambridge and it was decided then that the Centre for Crop Circle Studies should attempt to meet the hoaxers, the one mathematician or the six engineering students! Montague Keen received an assurance from the Vice-Chancellor of the University that no action would be taken against any student who 'confessed', he then appealed through the Varsity newspaper, which is circulated to about 10,000 college members, for the hoaxers to come forward.

The only response was a letter written to me in the New Year of 1992, in which the writer said *he* was the mathematician suspected of the hoax. He hadn't done it, but please could he have information about the formation for those in the Pure Mathematics faculty, who were extremely interested in it. When we met, his comments on the survey drawing were, "This isn't perfect. No mathematician would have made this. Perhaps it *was made* by some engineering students". He was, however, amazed by the photographs. The response of Stephen Hawking, one of the world's leading cosmologists from Cambridge University and author of the best selling *A Brief History of Time*, was "it was most certainly a hoax".

The Mandelbrot in the Corn

I visited the formation on Friday 16th August with some friends after work. We followed the farmer's directions, crossing the harvested fields in the car. Nothing could be seen at eye level, except for one field of ripened corn near Welches Wood, a small wood which could be seen from the road, and was on the cresting of the hill, rising from the shallow valley and the Icknield Way. The sun was low in the sky. We walked along the tractor tram-lines from the field boundary hedge on the south towards the wood — and stumbled into the most beautiful of formations. Our point of entry was at the cleft of the heart shape. The sun was now sinking fast, the light was intense, and the flattened wheat gleamed, the standing wheat was silhouetted like lace curtains around the rim. The division between each part of the formation was clearly defined by single stems of standing wheat. A delicacy that is hard to describe.

George Wingfield and his family travelled to Cambridge in response to my earlier message: "There's a beautiful formation — heart-shaped, with complications". I drew the formation for them on the kitchen table when they arrived and discovered then from George that it was a Mandelbrot Set. Until then I had been happy with the view that it was a mandala or labyrinth, with parallels in antiquity, found worldwide on ancient sites, and similar to one at Tintagel in Cornwall. They are symbols of spiritual development and initiation.[5] The deflection of the laid corn emphasised the pathway that could have been made as you followed the lines of a classical labyrinth.

However.

We visited the site that afternoon and sat in the formation, on the swirled corn. Around us was a wall of ripened wheat, interspersed with small swirled circles of corn. Tiny arable weeds had thrust their way through the stems of the laid wheat and were in flower: heartsease, scarlet pimpernel and fumitory. I had noticed this green-ness in other circles where these small plants had taken advantage of light as though the field had been harvested. George Wingfield was able to fly over the formation on Sunday, and other friends flew over in a microlite. Meanwhile I returned to the formation to photograph and complete my measuring survey. None of us knew how precious this time was to be!

The Formation Characteristics and Survey Details

The core of the formation was a round heart shape or *cardioid*, with precisely positioned circles around the perimeter. These were sym-metrically aligned with the axis. Tiny circles were dispersed between them and on the three large attached circles.

The characteristics familiar now to crop circles could be seen in the formation; the swirled clockwise and counter-clockwise patterns around a central node, a clearly-defined edge, and a wall of standing corn. The alignment to a tractor tram-line made use of this existing feature to give the connection between the main formation and the

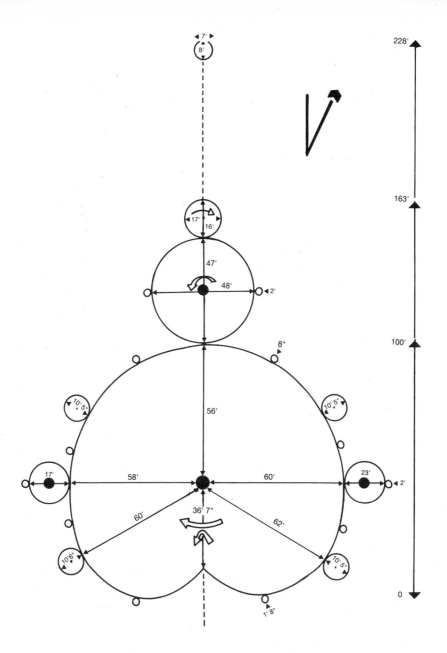

THE MANDELBROT CIPHER, which appeared on 10 August 1991 at Ickleton, 10 miles south of Cambridge, and within a mile of the Michael ley line and the Icknield Way. Scale drawing, showing magnetic north, by Beth Davis. (*O.S. Ref. TL 467414*)

outlier, or seed Mandelbrot. There was also an association with the nearby copse of trees and ancient burial sites seen from earlier aerial photographs in the next field to the east.

From the aerial photograph, the circular form of the cardioid can be seen clearly. The bands of concentric circles were laid outwards from the central node in a clockwise manner, slightly ovoid, in anticipation of the need to achieve the width of the cardioid, and then stretching or widening each band to conform with the shape of the two lobes and cleft. The lobes were unequal. This characteristic is common to large crop circle formations, almost as though a template was used, but was not exactly parallel to the ground surface during its execution. In this case, the lobe on the eastern side was larger than the other lobe. Each circle was similarly mis-shaped with the node off-centre. The walls of the formations and smaller circles were very precisely cut; the transition between the laid horizontal stems and the vertical stems had an almost mechanical quality. At the perimeter, a few clockwise stems were swept into the counter-clockwise lay of the attached circles. The most remarkable feature was the delicate fringe of standing corn between the perimeter circles, and each other, and the cardioid. The laying of the circles was so precise that at their junction, several plants graded to one plant and finally a single standing stem. Some single stems along the tramlines and seen particularly in the smallest seed circles are left standing from the time of the formation.

Each of the larger circles appeared almost like inverted saucers, to compensate for the thickness of the laid corn. The central nodes in each were clear of stems and were lightly dished into the soil. The smallest circles were less than two feet (0.6 m) in diameter, and the corn stems were buckled to form small clockwise and counter-clockwise nests. Each stem was bent above the ground, but did not appear to have been damaged or split.

Winter wheat in Cambridgeshire is usually harvested in the middle of August. A neighbouring farmer was busy harvesting peas in a nearby field, and said he thought that the crop was about 10 days away from harvest. At the time of the formation, the field was golden and had not suffered any wind damage. It was in perfect condition to be sculptured! The stems had been laid closely to the ground without any apparent distortion at the critical points near the cleft, where the tractor tram-line had been used to define the change of direction. The circle pattern began at 13'7" (4.9m) from the cleft of the cardioid. The transition, a little untidy at ground level, could be seen more clearly in the aerial photographs.

The compass bearing of the axis of the formation, from magnetic north, was 334°. The interval between each feature on the perimeter from the central node was approximately 30°. The formation had been divided into twelve equal segments with tiny circles between the larger circles bisecting a segment. I also dowsed these radials.

The Demise of the Formation

On Monday 19th August harvesting began, and the combine cut a single line through the axis of the Mandelbrot formation. This was photographed from the air by John Haddington, Patron of the Centre for Crop Circle Studies (see p. 35), and after the harvest by Dr David Wilson. The ground plan of the Mandelbrot survived. Later in the week contractors came in to bale the straw, and the bales were left for collection.

On the following Saturday, the son of the neighbouring farmer noticed smoke from a fire in the field. He telephoned the fire services and hurriedly got the ploughman working for the owner to plough around the Mandelbrot to contain the fire. The unharvested stems of corn were burning furiously. No one could explain how the fire had started; the hedge to the south and the copse were not touched. The flames were apparently fanned across the field by the prevailing wind into the Mandelbrot formation. Gossip in the local pubs implied that this was the work of the military or an outside agent. Who is to know? After the fire the Mandelbrot could still be seen clearly from the air, and on the ground it was sufficiently identifiable to be surveyed by Chris Phillips, John Sayes, Mathew Gregory and Michael Inns. The smallest circle escaped the fire and some stems of the wheat were photographed by Michael Inns. Later in September, I found no evidence of the fire in the deeply ploughed field.

NOTES

1. McNish, John, *Crop Circle Communique*, (Video) 1991.
2. *Cambridge Evening News*, August 15th, 16th, 22nd, 1991.
3. *ibid.*
4. Gleick, James, *Chaos*, Cardinal Books, 1988.
5. Purse, Jill, *The Mystic Spiral*, Thames & Hudson, 1974.

The Cipher of Chaos

George Wingfield

*"For the Snark's a peculiar creature that won't
Be caught in a commonplace way.
Do all that you know, and try all that you don't:
Not a chance must be wasted today."*

Lewis Carroll *The Hunting of the Snark*

On a day in late summer 1985, a number of us made our way wearily down the mountainside on the north coast of Knoydart, in the Scottish Highlands. We had arrived that morning by boat from Inverie, and apart from the occasional croft, there was no sign of human habitation. In this wide vista of sea and mountains, a Buccaneer jet which flew noisily along Loch Hourn, was our sole reminder of the outside world.

Exhausted and thirsty after an unsuccessful day's stalking, we descended towards a tiny croft near the sea. We had been directed to this cottage by our ghillie (gamekeeper), who said that a young American had come to live there, seeking solitude, and to avoid being drafted to Vietnam. With me were my wife, Gloria, and John Haddington, together with some other friends. We knocked and were ushered courteously inside.

If we had failed in our pursuit of one kind of beast on the mountain, another creature of a most exotic and intriguing kind lay in wait for us in that crofter's cottage. It was one with which we were totally unfamiliar, but which has had a profound effect on western scientific thinking and on man's perception of the world since that time. On the screen of our new-found American friend's personal computer a strange shape was gradually developing, line by line. In the centre lay a great black heart symmetrically surrounded by a number of smaller circles, with its surface covered in tiny nodules and spiky protuberances. This was the first time any of us had set eye on the Mandelbrot Set.

Explanation of what this strange and unexpected beast on the highland PC monitor actually represented was not easy to follow for the uninitiated. But the current edition of Scientific American (August 1985) lay beside the computer and a brief perusal of its cover story, entitled '*Exploring the Mandelbrot Set*'[1], provided our first cursory introduction to the science of fractals. From then on John Haddington and I were both hooked on what proved to be the key to a magical new world of infinite intricacy, beauty and colour.

The slow personal computers of the mid-1980s were hardly sufficient to perform the enormous number-crunching operations required to disclose the full detail and complexity of fractals. But in seven years computer technology has advanced in leaps and bounds, and now it is quite within the scope of a home computer to rapidly calculate and display the incredible intricacies of the Mandelbrot Set, on a high-resolution colour graphics screen. A whole new world, the realm of mathematical chaos, has now been opened up and is familiar to millions.

The Mandelbrot Set

The Mandelbrot Set sits like some huge black abstract spider, at the centre of a web of unimaginable complexity. In fact it resides within a two-dimensional sheet of numbers known to mathematicians as the Complex Plane. Using a high-powered computer to calculate values resulting from a simple repeated operation, for each point in this plane, it is found that the complex numbers within the black outline of the Mandelbrot remain finite, whereas those outside it flee to infinity. Close to the boundary of the Set the calculated points dance about in a frenzy indicating the onset of instability. The surface seems to bubble and boil as the computer attempts to quantify these co-ordinates, which hover on the brink of chaos.

The boundary of the Set represents the dividing line, infinitely long, between order within and chaos without. Intermediate states, where points in the complex plane flee more gradually to infinity, are arbitrarily coloured purple, blue, green, red, etc., in accordance with the degree of instability, giving rise to the 'solar flares' or dendrites, which festoon the spiky surface of the black Set itself. All these coloured regions, which are not truly within the Mandelbrot Set itself, can be arbitrarily displayed or excluded from the computer-generated picture. It should be noted that the characteristic shape of the Mandelbrot is probably something far more fundamental still, since it occurs in other fractal formulae, such as a Newtonian equation for the solving of polynomials.

In speaking of *complex numbers*, we are using a technical mathematical expression to denote numbers with two components, known as the *real* and *imaginary* parts. Again this is a technical expression used to define the number's two components, or coordinates, and to give it a fractional dimension. The 'imaginary' component contains the factor 'i', which denotes the square-root of minus-one, something considered impossible or unreal in elementary mathematics. Hence the word 'imaginary'. It is the use of this abstract value 'i' which opens up the whole new discipline of fractals.

Rather than launch into a lengthy mathematical dissertation, I shall assume that the basis for computation of the Mandelbrot Set is understood by numerate readers, and accepted by those who are less numerate. The Set is named after Benoit Mandelbrot, a research fellow at IBM's Thomas J. Watson Research Center in Yorktown Heights, New York State. A distinguished mathematician, he was able to explore the field of mathematical sets using high-powered computers which were introduced by IBM in the late 1960s and the 1970s. Traditional mathematicians clung to the logic which they insisted should be formalised as rigorous proofs for every new proposition. Mandelbrot, in the style of Poincaré a hundred years earlier, cared less for rigour than for results. With the computer as his chosen instrument he began to explore the phenomenon of scaling, discovering an unexpected quality of order among apparent chaos. The direction of this research took many turns but his approach remained that so long as it deepened the understanding of nature, it was significant, whether or not the conclusions could be rigorously proven.

Mandelbrot moved beyond the concept of normal dimensions 0, 1, 2, 3 . . . to what seemed then an impossibility: fractional dimensions. In 1975 he coined the expression *fractal geometry*. In particular the boundary of the Mandelbrot Set is a fractal, but it is also very much more.

Let us take a closer look at this boundary, which is infinitely long and connects all parts of the Mandelbrot Set, including many islands which lie at a distance from the main cardioid and its attendant circles. These islands, enclaves of stability within a sea of chaos, are generally of minute size compared with the main Mandelbrot. On computer, we can also magnify areas of the complex plane to show additional detail of what lies in any particular neck of the woods. Successive magnifications, which necessitate recalculation of all the points in the area designated, and may take considerable time, reveal extraordinary and beautiful detail hidden everywhere close to the boundary of the main Set.

These magnifications can in theory proceed indefinitely into the infinite recesses of this, the most complex object in mathematics. In practice some computers can achieve magnification factors of billions of times the original scale. At each level we find tiny replicas of the original Mandelbrot, always with the same familiar black shape, like some monstrous seed-potato covered in tiny protuberances. These baby Mandelbrots are all attached to the original Set by the finest filaments which themselves show an unbelievable wealth of the most delicate detail. And the baby Mandelbrots, when magnified to full size, reveal the existence of still further black dots lurking at a distance from their surface, which are yet further baby Mandelbrots, whose identity is only realised when additional magnification operations are performed. Thus, in the immortal words of Jonathan Swift:-

So, naturalists observe, a flea
Hath smaller fleas that on him prey;
And these have smaller fleas to bite 'em,
And so proceed ad infinitum.

In this abstract microscopic wonderland, made visible by modern technology, we find whorls and spirals connected to curlicues of unimaginable delicacy. Looking at the surface of the great black seed, which is the Mandelbrot Set, we find each tiny wart closely resembles the parent Set. But if one zooms in for a closer look at these minute shapes, endless different patterns appear. There are spirals and tendrils of the finest gossamer, each precisely formed. These curlicues look not so much like crystal structures as like plants which have grown with a regularity amounting to perfection. Some resemble the tails of sea-horses, others are like spiralling sea-shells or the petals of some intricate flower. Magnifying a whorl, one finds bridges and islands connected by endless strands of bejewelled filigree. A tiny black dot embedded in this incredible micro-world proves on magnification to be yet another replica of the Mandelbrot Set, not identical, but similar in form. On zooming further and further into this strange infinity we meet countless such objects always similar, but different.

Each time, a profusion of colour and complexity fills the screen, stretching away into infinite vistas of order within chaos. All this results from the simplest of mathematical formulae.

After long contemplation of this magical world, now accessible to anyone with a reasonably powerful modern computer, we must ask what connection there is here with the 'real' and material world which we all inhabit. The most striking facet of this newly-revealed wonderland of the Mandelbrot Set is an internal consistency which extends to all levels of magnification, and indeed seems to mirror life itself. The seed of order within chaos is the distinctive black Mandelbrot, found, like Jonathan Swift's fleas, at every level of magnification. The principle of *as above, so below* is illustrated a billion-fold and more within this abstract world.

The analogies with our world can be extended to other respects as well. That the black Mandelbrot 'seeds', on close inspection, are not found to be identical seems a clue in itself. Superficially alike, they are like humans seen from a distance, each different when seen close to. So too the whorls and spirals which proliferate in every direction at all levels of magnification. Nevertheless, within this realm of apparent chaos there is a consistency which permeates every recess of these infinite vistas, in a way that is analogous to life itself. The overall blueprint for the Mandelbrot Set in its infinite layers of complexity is entirely reminiscent of the blueprint which controls the pattern of life on earth and perhaps of life throughout the universe. With the Mandelbrot this blueprint is described by simple mathematical rules, and with life the rules of birth, growth and death are similarly encoded within our DNA, the biological building-block of living matter.

The Cipher at Ickleton

Six years after John Haddington and I had first stared in surprise at that peculiar shape on the computer screen in Knoydart, another such cipher lay waiting for us in the fields of Cambridgeshire, totally unexpected, just as the first had been. In mid-August 1991 I received a telephone call from Beth Davis, who lives near Huntingdon, to say that a strange heart-shaped formation had appeared near Ickleton, ten miles south of Cambridge. "A heart with complications", she added, noting that it was encompassed by 'pendant' circles. I made a mental note of this, but did not think that it was of any special significance, since at that time crop circle formations of all shapes and sizes had been appearing up and down the country, especially in the Marlborough area of Wiltshire.

On August 17th however I had gone to look at various formations in Northamptonshire and Cambridgeshire, and later called on Beth. I was in no way prepared for what we found. From the lane running beside the field one simply could not tell that there was any sort of crop formation in the wheat on the brow of this hill, barely half a mile from the ancient track of the Icknield Way, which here coincides with the so-called St Michael Line, which runs from Cornwall to Norfolk. It was no surprise to me that, yet again, here was a formation in close proximity to the line of the St Michael current — a dowsable line of earth energy described by Hamish Miller and Paul Broadhurst in their book *The Sun and the Serpent*[2]. Other circles had been found near this line, and near the line of the Mary current, which passes through Silbury Hill and the henge at Wandlebury, Cambridgeshire, where circles were found in 1990.

Accompanied by Beth, Gloria and my son Rupert, we went into the field and entered the huge heart-shaped formation along a tram-line. The initial suspicion that this was indeed a representation of the Mandelbrot Set soon crystallised into certainty as we examined the huge formation in the quiet of this remote cornfield. Photographing the different features of this Mandelbrot, and sketching the layout of the various circles, enabled comparisons with the diagrams in various textbooks at a later time. But there was no doubt what this formation was meant to be, and the significance of this vast cipher, if it was genuine, was not lost on us.

One is sometimes criticised for being too willing to accept crop formations as 'genuine', before painstaking examination and research has been completed. It is a fair criticism, but with the Mandelbrot at Ickleton the sheer perfection of the lay of the crop was quite apparent to all those who actually *saw* it at ground level. The wheat was swept flat with a flow which showed no trace of the irregular jerky movements so often apparent in hoaxed circles. Even after five days, few people had visited the site, and there was minimal sign of damage to the crop. The tiny circles tangential to the perimeter of the great cardioid were minute works of art in themselves: neat unbroken swirls of scarcely 18 inches diameter touched the main body of the Mandelbrot with confident precision and immaculate circularity.

MANDELBROT CIRCLE DETAILS. *top*: A western satellite, showing delicate separating 'curtain'. *left*: Edge of large cardiodid, showing weaving of floor pattern and a small satellite. *right*: The northernmost satellite. (Photos by Beth Davis).

Reactions to the Mandelbrot

Human reaction to a bewildering event of this nature is often entirely predictable. To most of those unfamiliar with the crop circle phenomenon, and the way in which it has progressed and evolved over the last few years, incredulity inevitably gives way to suspicion, if not hostility. They are being asked to accept something which is quite clearly *much too much*. "Of course, it has to be a hoax" is the reaction. "It couldn't be anything else . . . could it?"

Such thoughts were the usual reactions of those unfamiliar with the phenomenon, and this of course embraced the whole gamut from farm labourer to university don. Implicit in this reaction was a willingness to accept the agency of a natural phenomenon, however weird, but a total reluctance to even consider the alternative possibility, the existence of a non-human intelligence, whatever form that might take.

The Ickleton Mandelbrot was indeed a watershed. Here for the first time was a clearly recognisable mathematical shape, and one which does not occur in nature, so far as we know. Not only was the Circle-maker intelligence testing us — it was saying that this intelligence was of the very highest order. Here was the crunch: would even those cereologists who had followed the phenomenon throughout its innumerable twists and turns be able to take this one on board? Many were unable to do so. Together with the sceptics and all of those encumbered with half-baked theories, they fled towards the supposed refuge of rationality.

Its proximity to Cambridge University could certainly be construed in different ways. First, for those who could accept this unprecedented development, in a phenomenon which has always been linked to human consciousness, this positioning was quite in keeping. Much of Chaos Theory and the new science of fractals had been developed at Cambridge, and the Mandelbrot Set would by 1991 be a familiar object to large numbers of students, especially in the science faculties.

The sceptics would bolster their case with exactly the same consideration. Of course the Mandelbrot was near Cambridge, since mathematical students would inevitably choose this design when carrying out such a hoax in the local cropfields!

A further rumour, given currency by *Cropwatcher*[4] magazine, was that Arthur C. Clark knew who had made the Ickleton Mandelbrot. Indeed, Clark has said as much, and he even named the person he believed the culprit. This was Cade Roux, a Cambridge mathematician, who corresponded with Beth and denied the rumours.

At the time of the formation, I contacted Dr Mandelbrot himself in Yorktown Heights, New York State, sending an account of what we had found, together with a number of aerial photographs. He wrote back expressing great interest, but was careful also to be entirely non-committal as to the origin of the Ickleton cipher. Concurrent with my correspondence, poor Mandelbrot was bombarded with enquiries and opinions from journalists and scientists alike, concerning the event, and this course taken by him was undoubtedly prudent. This slightly sceptical public stance appears to be a *de rigeur* attitude for most scientists, who fear the scorn of their fellows if they were to accept anything out of line with modern reductionist thinking.

Destruction of the Mandelbrot

Whatever one thinks about the origin of this enormous cipher, there was no denying that it constituted a work of art. The aesthetic beauty of the perfectly-incised cardioid and its attendant circles is clearly seen. But all things of beauty have a transitory existence and are soon swept away.

On that Saturday afternoon in August I was acutely aware that the crop was due to be harvested any day, and it was unlikely that the Mandelbrot's fate could be postponed.

I needed to fly over the site. After a day of delays and innumerable telephone calls,I was told that the flight previously arranged had to be cancelled. Furious and frustrated, we drove to Sibson where we were able to hire another plane. Together with Gloria and Rupert we set off to film the Mandelbrot, flying by way of Guyhirn in the Fens where there were two other strange crop formations which I wanted to photograph. Over Guyhirn there was initially no sign of the formations we sought. Then Rupert spotted a mis-shapen quincunx in a distant field and our pilot turned towards it. Below us two combine harvesters were moving steadily through the field and had already swallowed one of the crop formations we were after.

After photographing the quincunx we flew in the direction of Cambridge. The light was fading somewhat and the sky was hazy. However luck smiled on us once more, and on reaching Ickleton, there below lay the great symbol of chaos in the corn. Two tiny figures, one dressed in scarlet and the other in black and white could be seen standing in the cardioid. Although the fields on every side had been cut by the harvesters, that containing the Mandelbrot still stood unscathed. Several aerial circuits later I had taken a whole reel of film.

Later that evening the whole fantastic implication of the Ickleton Mandelbrot came home to me. If what I had seen and photographed was a true formation — and I had no doubt that it was — the significance of this extraordinary event could not be overstated. This thing *should* be the principal item on national television news. It *should* be examined and recorded by scientists in the greatest detail before it was harvested, and that, of course, should be postponed until such time as this could be done thoroughly. It should be something that everyone was made aware of, and if that could be done it might at last stir the imagination and consciousness of the sleeping masses.

But who could one tell? Certainly not the media, whose perception of crop circle matters, even in the days prior to the Doug'n'Dave scam, was little short of juvenile. I resolved to try one or two Cambridge academics, but this was totally without success. They were away or unavailable. Next I telephoned a whole list of people who, I knew, were interested in crop circles, and managed to reach just a few. Amid mounting frustration, I tried desperately to convey the importance of what we had found at Ickleton and pleaded with some at least to go and see the great cipher before it was destroyed. Some of those I spoke to replied *"What is a Mandelbrot?"*, and left me stumbling over my words in a futile effort to explain. One recipient of my calls was the spokesman for a Japanese television team, which had just spent several weeks filming the circles and carrying out an expensive surveillance project in Wiltshire. Unimpressed by my frenzied attempt to convey the significance of the Mandelbrot, he thanked me kindly and said that the Japanese had spent their budget and could not fit in a trip to Cambridgeshire.

After two hours of fruitless telephone calls I sank back in despair. I had often thought that if ever an alien spaceship landed in Hyde Park, London, the British would not just fail to notice it, but would refuse to acknowledge it, even if it put down right next to them. "Oh, that? It's just some television programme they're making, I think. Well, even if it isn't, it's not important anyway". And if one is too insistent, the reply would always be "Well it has to be a hoax, doesn't it?" Although this is hardly a fair analogy, I think that the Ickleton Mandelbrot was an event of quite extraordinary significance and yet it was met, in general, with customary British apathy.

There were two, however, who did respond to my urgent bidding, and all was not lost. David Parker hired a plane the next morning and flew to Ickleton. His amazing photographs of the wheaten Mandelbrot are shown in these pages. John Haddington hurried down from Scotland, taking a train to Peterborough and hiring the same Cessna as me at Sibson. When he reached the formation at 1.40pm on that Monday, just one week after its initial discovery, he found that the harvesters had driven right through the great heart. A single swath had been made straight along the centre line of the formation, probably no more than an hour before he reached it. The combine had then been stopped and its driver had gone for lunch!

What Mean These Signs?

Exactly a year before the appearance of the Ickleton Mandelbrot, a certain Martyn Hughes (of Highworth, Wilts) had written a letter to *New Scientist* magazine (11th August 1990),[5] which had been entitled *Corn and Chaos*. It read: "*The formations of corn circles are growing in complexity each summer. How long before we see a complete Mandelbrot Set?*"

Other aficionados of the crop circles also yearned for such a cipher of chaos in the crops, and this sort of expectation is entirely in character with the response of the phenomenon, as I have written in *Crop Circles — Harbingers of World Change*. With the Mandelbrot we have at last an entirely recognisable symbol.[6] Nevertheless its meaning is not something that can be conveyed in just a few words.

Like the formation at Barbury Castle the Ickleton figure does contain some slight imperfections. The absence of 'solar flares' or dendrites is not an imperfection, since these are not seen in a computer-generated set of low potential, rather than a high potential one which emphasises dendrites and spikiness. The most noticeable imperfection is the placement of the small isolated circle on the main axis. In a true Mandelbrot this should lie rather further from the rest of the Set, and should in fact be a small replica of the Mandelbrot Set rather than a circle; proportionately it should be quite a bit smaller than this small circle on the centre line.

With a computer-generated Mandelbrot the most prominent of the small circles at the sides of the large circle over the cardioid are those in the '10 o'clock' and '2 o'clock' positions. With the Ickleton figure the small circles at '9 o'clock' and '3 o'clock' are more prominent. Similar criticism may also be directed at the placement of some of the tiny circles attached to the great cardioid. The smallest diameter for any of the tiny circles has to be of the same order of magnitude as the average length of a stalk of corn for obvious reasons, so one would not expect to find detail smaller than a foot or two.

Despite these imperfections and the constraints imposed by the medium, the wheat Mandelbrot is a remarkable feat, whatever its origin. I have frequently said that one can never be 100% sure of a crop circle's authenticity, since one did not see it form. There is always some chance that it was created by a human agency and doubtless, people will lay claim to its construction. But all those who want to prove me wrong and claim that they made the Ickleton Mandelbrot will have to produce a formation of equal size and perfection, in total darkness, before they can be believed!

So how are we to interpret this magnificent symbol in the wheat? Many previous circles have been quincunxes which are a common form of mandala. These express the totality of the universe and they express the balance between the elements of which it consists. One variant of the quincunx, or the *quinta essentia* of the ancients, symbolises the four material elements: earth, water, air and fire. The 'fifth essence', which was symbolised by the central circle, represents the life-force.

In exploring the hidden meaning of such symbols as the quincunx, the central motif is often depicted as the seed from which the outer circles grow. This theme is touched upon by Brian Grist in chapter four. The process of creation is seen as the transformation of chaos into order. In the language of *Genesis*, the spirit of God (or *logos*) moves on the face of the deep. This initiates the creation of the four elements, or the forming of the material world. Chaos has been changed into order. But order is transient and will at some stage revert to chaos. The harmony of order is no more than a delicate balance which will, like the crop circles themselves, be swept away at the appointed time. Modern cosmology is based upon an analogue of this concept. In the 'Big Bang' theory of creation, all matter, and indeed the dimensions of space itself, is held to have been created from the unimaginable explosion of an infinitely dense and infinitely small 'super-atom'. Take your pick as to which version of Genesis, ancient or modern, you prefer!

This ancient theme finds modern scientific expression in the Second

Law of Thermodynamics, which states that the entropy of a closed system always remains constant or increases. Here *entropy* is defined as a measure of the probability of degree of disorder. Order, and indeed life itself, arises out of chaos as a result of the life-force. But it will return to chaos. The ancient mystics saw the end of the world as the reversal of the creation process. The four elements which constitute the material universe return into a state of chaos. The apocalypse describes this engulfing of the world by fire — the fourth element, fire, being in fact a representation of celestial fire, from which the sun and stars are supposedly made. And the chaos to which all is returned is then transformed again into pure spirit, or the Mind of God.

Such apocalyptic visions may seem unfashionable in the modern scientific world but nevertheless the balance between order and chaos is evident to scientists in both microcosm and macrocosm. This is what the Mandelbrot represents and it is a stark and meaningful expression, symbolic of the duality of nature and totally consistent with the quincunx symbols which preceded it. Whether this great cipher which appeared in 1991 in the fields at Ickleton manages to penetrate human consciousness, any more than the symbols which came earlier, is something that remains to be seen.

NOTES

1. *Exploring the Mandelbrot Set*, Scientific American, August 1985.
2. Miller Hamish, & Broadhurst, Paul, *The Sun and the Serpent*, Pendragon Press, Cornwall, 1989.
3. Letters, *New Scientist* and *The Circular*, Summer 1991.
4. *The Cropwatcher* 1991.
5. *New Scientist*, 11th August 1990.
6. Bartholomew Alick, ed. *Crop Circles — Harbingers of World Change*, Gateway Books, 1991.

The Great Cipher at Barbury Castle

George Wingfield

"Symbols are a means of explaining our reality, but reality is always beyond the symbol" Father Bede Griffiths, Winchester 1992.

The most spectacular of all the 1991 pictograms appeared in a wheat-field near Barbury Castle on July 17th. Barbury Castle is an Iron Age hill fort five miles south of Swindon, capping Barbury Hill, part of the Marlborough Downs. Across the face of Barbury Hill, close to the field where the pictogram appeared, runs the ancient track known as the Ridgeway. Three miles further south on this track, near the Avebury Sanctuary, during that summer, many crop-watchers had positioned themselves night after night to watch the fields and the skies.

On the night of July 16/17th a small group of watchers, consisting of Brian Grist, Gary Hardwick and Alison Baggot, did indeed observe something remarkable in the skies, if not in the fields. From a vantage point to the west of Avebury they watched a number of pulsing lights move silently across the sky, and what they saw is described in chapter five. On the morning of 17th July, Brian called to tell me about their experiences. He was clearly shaken by these events and likened what they had seen to a sequence from the film *Close Encounters of the Third Kind*. There were two reports by other crop-watchers that night, of lights seen in the sky from where they stood near Silbury Hill.

At the time of my telephone conversation with Brian Grist, neither of us had any inkling of the appearance of the great Barbury Castle pictogram. News of that came soon afterwards in a telephone call from Nick Bailey. At 9am that morning he had flown with photographer Richard Wintle, who wanted to take pictures of the insect-like crop formations near Stonehenge. As they circled in Nick's Robinson 22 helicopter near Draycot airfield, before heading for Stonehenge, they caught sight of the great pictogram. They could hardly believe their eyes as they stared down at the huge pattern below. Nick knew that the field, just two miles from his home airfield, had been blank when he flew over it, as it was getting dark the previous evening. Now, barely twelve hours later, it contained the largest crop formation he had ever seen.

"I think that you had better come and have a look at this", said Nick Bailey on the telephone. "It's quite extraordinary, and unlike any of the other formations". I replied that he really didn't have to go to these lengths to get me to fly again, even though I had flown in his helicopter just three days before. "I'll be along as soon as I can get away."

The Barbury Triangle from the Air

A few hours later I sat strapped in the tiny red and white helicopter as we flew over Barbury Castle, peering down, with utter disbelief, at the vast hieroglyph in the green wheat-field below. This was indeed quite unlike anything which had gone before. The huge triangular design was like a great maze, and by this time there were people in every part of it. Yet from the air its sharp geometric outline was nothing short of perfection — as can be seen from photographs taken on that day.

The great equilateral triangle, with sides of about sixty yards, encompassed a massive double-ringed circle, but with the outer ring crossing beyond the bounds of the triangle's sides. Perched on each corner of the huge triangle were circular devices, each different, and each about 27 yards across. At one corner was a spiral ratchet pathway, twisting outward from a small central circle. Next a plain ring pierced by a straight radial pathway, from an apex of the triangle. And lastly a sun-wheel in which six curving, equally-spaced arcs spread out from the centre to the containing ring. From the central circle of the pictogram three straight pathways ran out to the apexes of the great triangle, bisecting its angles. These lines gave the overall design the appearance of a three-dimensional shape — that of a tetrahedron or pyramid — represented two-dimensionally.

The sheer articulation of this precise design removed any residual doubt anyone may have had, that this agriglyph could possibly have resulted from any natural phenomenon. Here was unmistakable proof of intelligent design, whether of human or non-human origin.

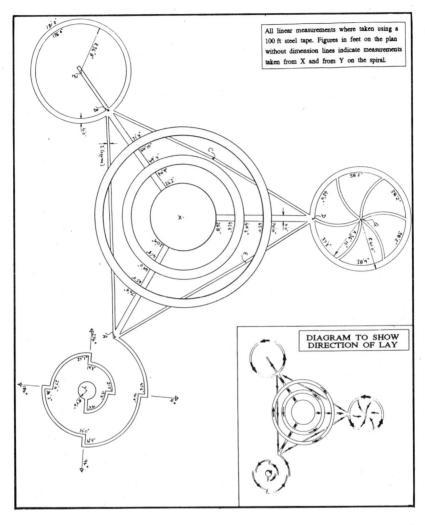

All linear measurements where taken using a
100 ft steel tape. Figures in feet on the plan
without dimension lines indicate measurements
taken from X and from Y on the spiral.

DIAGRAM TO SHOW
DIRECTION OF LAY

BARBURY CASTLE. This three-dimensional tetrahedron, is a cipher of sacred geometry *par excellence*, and contrary to the Circlemakers' usual procedure, it had no precedents. Instead, it seemed to foretell themes-to-come. The top circle is a half-complete six-petal flower; the lower left circle comes in the later 'whale' formations; the lower right is a labyrinth exactly 333ft long (a mystical number, though hardly an international measure!). It was oriented exactly due north. It can yield hours of contemplative reward. This configuration marked a quantum shift in the evolution of the phenomenon, and implies a clear philosophical message. (J.F. Langrish drawing).

And yet the scale of this masterpiece, and its apparent lack of errors, was such that it was hard to conceive that it could have been furtively made during the hours of darkness by any band of hoaxers, however expert or determined.

Looking down from above, one was inevitably struck by the incongruity of what lay below. Here was a massive artefact laid out in all its complexity in this green wheat-field, and no one had the slightest clue as to its origin. Puzzled and incredulous people moved like ants in the sunshine below us, exploring every corner of the maze. I shot frame after frame of film from every angle, knowing that this thing of beauty would soon be mutilated by human visitation, its pristine lines trampled and destroyed. Even as I filmed, one of three girls at one apex stumbled, and fell into the standing crop, disfiguring part of the design.

Preshute Down

Eventually we flew on, and within a minute we were over a field just a mile to the south, where a second pictogram had appeared that morning, on Preshute Down. This was more orthodox in style, but nevertheless quite remarkable. Here was a long design consisting of interconnected circles and rings with a device like a three-fingered 'hand', protruding from one end. Again the sharp outline of the pictogram in the green wheat demonstrated a precision and articulation, which would be quite unachievable by basic hoaxing methods. We could see French cereologist Yves Chosson at the edge of the field below, where he had just carried out a survey.

The proximity of the Preshute pictogram to the Barbury Castle one, and its contemporaneous appearance, gave every indication that they were produced by the same agency, whatever that might be. Then there were the strange lights in the sky seen by Brian, Gary and Alison the previous night. Yet any explanation in conventional terms seemed totally inadequate.

This pictogram presented another puzzle, unlike that at Barbury Castle. The whole wheat-field was criss-crossed with tiny wavy tracks unlike any I had seen before in my aerial surveys. They might be the tracks of small animals, but many of them appeared to end in the standing crop as if whatever had caused them had simply vanished. The tracks were centred on the pictogram and many of them led out from it almost as if they had 'disembarked' from whatever had been there.

Plates 1 & 2. Landscapes at Ickleton, near Cambridge, looking north.
(Top: David Parker/Science Photo Library; bottom: George Wingfield)

Plate 3. THE MANDELBROT, an
unmistakable clone of the set of
that name, familiar to modern
chaos theoreticians, appeared on
12 August 1991, at Ickleton,
10 miles south of Cambridge.
(David Parker/Science Photo Library)

Plate 4. This photographer arrived
just too late! The combine harvester,
in a rather pointed act of defiance,
has made a pass through the centre
of the Mandelbrot.
(John Haddington)

Plate 5. Looking south towards the
main cardioid circle, showing the
beautiful 'lace curtain' effect, where
the smaller circles delicately touch
the edge of the larger circle.
(Elizabeth Wilson)

6.

7.

Plate 6. THE BARBURY CASTLE configuration, which formed on 17th July 1991, was like this for only 24 hours before suffering rain damage.
(Centre: Calyx Photo Services)

Plates 7, 8 & 9. Detail of the centre and two outlying circles of the Barbury Castle configuration. Pole shots. *(Busty Taylor)*

10.

11.

12.

Plate 10. BARBURY CASTLE, an iron age fort near Swindon, Wiltshire, stands above the Ridgeway ancient trackway and the remarkable configuration. It is thought an ancient 'White Horse' graced the slope in between.
(George Wingfield)

Plate 11. THE SERPENT at Froxfield near Hungerford, mid-August 1991. The only one of its kind. The pathways had strong dowsable energy counter-flows. Notice the discontinuities.
(Jürgen Krönig)

Plate 12. The brush that painted this Serpent used a marvellously flowing form. Helicopter shot.
(Jürgen Krönig)

Plate 13. This corner of the Serpent looks like a fast-flowing stream. (*Jürgen Krönig*)

Plate 14. A river of energy flowed through the over-ripe wheat. (*Jürgen Krönig*)

13.

14.

The tracks were just a few inches wide and were irregular. They could have been made by foxes, and there was certainly a fox earth beside the field; but it did not look that way. It looked as if some energy, perhaps similar to the circle-making agency, had fizzled about like an erratic firework, and spent itself in the wheat. Maybe there is some ordinary explanation for the tracks, which will become plain in due course.

The Barbury Triangle at Ground Level

Later that day I had a chance to examine the Barbury Castle pictogram at ground level, and here again I was struck with its geometric precision. This agriglyph paid no heed to tractor tram-lines in the field; it was formed with a confidence and definiteness quite unlike the early pictograms of the preceding year, which relied heavily on the tram-lines, and often incorporated them as part of the pattern. The 'gap-seeking' tendency, described by Andrews and Delgado in *Circular Evidence*,[1] indicative of a weak, uncertain circle-scribing agency, was no longer to be found in the Wiltshire pictograms of 1991. This new boldness of form was particularly apparent at Barbury.

In fact many other characteristics of earlier circles and pictograms were entirely missing at Barbury Castle. Had one been trying to explain the formation in such terms, one would have been highly perplexed. Such reasoning could obviously lead one to think this was a hoax. But since the evolution of the circles has become an undoubted fact in the last few years, this new development should not be entirely surprising. It is consistent with the bold geometric development seen in all the 1991 Wiltshire pictograms.

The extended triangular form was also something to which we were unused. There had been triangles previously, but only triangles filled out from initial circles, and not drawn out like this with straight and narrow pathways. Also the central circle and its first annular ring were swept anti-clockwise, which is very unusual, though not unknown. And the swirl of this central circle was concentric, rather than spiralling outward, which is the lay most commonly seen — though this is not unknown. Lays of all sorts including the straight lays within each quadrant of the 1989 'swastika' circle were certainly a possibility. But, to anyone seeking a mechanistic explanation for the circles phenomenon, this dramatic new event at Barbury Castle was very difficult to take. If certain circles refused to fit one's cherished theory, then for some those circles obviously had to be fakes.

Genuine or Hoax?

In the pictogram that evening I met Dr Terence Meaden, who looked concerned. I said that surely this formation could never have been the result of an atmospheric vortex, and he seemed extremely thoughtful. He did not like it, he said, and remarked on the fact that there were broken stalks in the formation. There were indeed a few, which was hardly surprising, considering how many people had already been in the formation, and how I had even seen some of them falling about in it. Later information showed that the farmer's children had played in the pictogram during the morning, and from the air I had seen a large metal ladder belonging to Meaden's group being moved around the formation while they examined it.

Later a team from National Geographic magazine (Washington DC) interviewed Meaden and myself in the great pictogram. I said that all the indications were that the pictogram was genuine, insofar as most of its characteristics were similar to what we had seen previously. If that was the case, the implication of intelligent design was irresistible. He responded that the implication of intelligent design was there, "but it looks to me as if this one is probably human". Who would he suggest did it, if it was done by humans? "Nobody would be able to answer that sort of question. It would be somebody with a motive, who wanted to play tricks on both you and I simultaneously, perhaps".

The later statement by Terence Meaden in *Cropwatcher*[2] magazine, that "virtually every stem — millions of them — was broken or snapped, and many of the stems, numbering thousands, were broken in two or three places along the stem" is completely untrue, and does not represent what we saw in the Barbury Castle formation. We had looked for broken stems, and he had found some, but the assertion that there were 'millions' is not just hyperbole, but a fiction which does not correspond to what we saw. The lay of the crop and its condition was similar to that seen in most other crop circles, and the dowsable pattern, later checked by several experts, was entirely consistent with other formations of 1991. One person who was possibly the first to enter the pictogram, Mr Lowes, described the laid crop at that time as unbroken and perfect.

On that evening, most of those who were there agreed that no one could possibly have produced such a vast and complex geometric design during the hours of darkness. Farmer John White, on whose land the pictogram lay, said "No one could have done that. It definitely wasn't there last night". Even Dr Meaden was reported in the *Western Daily Press* to have subscribed to this view, initially. But if this formation were genuine, it spelled the end of the plasma vortex theory, and subsequently many attempts have been made by supporters of this theory to present the Barbury Castle pictogram as a hoax.

The Pictogram Devastated

Later on the same night, when everyone else had eventually gone home, Richard Beaumont (of *Kindred Spirit* magazine) and I sat under the night sky, in the centre of the spiral ratchet of the great pictogram, and contemplated the meaning of this huge cipher, which bore silent testimony to its bizarre origins. The whole formation seemed to fizz with an almost tangible energy — though many will say this was our imagining.

All was quiet, and we saw none of the strange lights in the sky that had been seen on the previous night. In the small hours the rain started to fall, and this eventually drove us to seek refuge in our cars and to abandon our crop-watch. The storm strengthened as the night progressed, and the rain beat down on the crop with a relentless fury. The damage to the Barbury pictogram caused by this storm mutilated a great work of art, and, combined with the damage of human visitation over the next two weeks, reduced the formation to a ragged and barely-recognisable mess. It had retained its original striking symmetry for barely 24 hours, but this was enough to capture that beauty on film.

The very definite symbolism of the Barbury pictogram is something which can and will generate any number of articles and books. It is something which has already produced remarkable results, and not ones that seem to be in any way contrived. John Michell has analysed the sacred geometry of the configuration, and discovered relationships which amount to divine revelation, no less. (See *The Cerealogist*, August 1991.)[3] Brian Grist writes, in this book, of the startling correspondence between the Barbury triangle and certain alchemical symbols, which are found in ancient hermetic texts. This link is very compelling too, and again we are given seemingly unmistakable interpretation of the devices on the triangle.

It is for each of us to find what the Barbury cipher represents, and that meaning is most likely something which we hold within us. Perhaps its very *existence* is sufficient to make its message clear. This will, of course, be lost to many, who can only make denials of any higher meaning, and a denial of any intelligence other than our own: the material world is the only reality that can be allowed, so far as they are concerned. But to the rest of us, the very existence of the Barbury pictogram, albeit transient and tantalisingly brief, was sufficient evidence of intelligence or consciousness, beyond our own, and gradually that suspicion is turning to a certainty.

NOTES

1. Delgado, Pat and Andrews, Colin, *Circular Evidence*. Bloomsbury, 1989.
2. *Cropwatcher*, 1991.
2. *Cerealogist*, August 1991.

Alchemy and Chaos at Barbury Castle

Brian Grist

A Mystery or a Hoax?

"*Right, now explain this one . . .* " ran the headline of a newspaper report[1] on the discovery of one of the most astonishing and genuinely awe-inspiring crop formations ever to have materialised in the fields of Britain. Formed on the night of July 16th/17th 1991, beneath the steep slopes of an Iron Age hill-fort beside the ancient Ridgeway on the northern edge of Wiltshire's Marlborough Downs, the Barbury Castle formation was entirely without precedent in the history of the phenomenon and, as such, took just about everybody involved in the 'mystery' completely by surprise.

Such was the visual impact of this extraordinary complex of straight lines and circles (described by the press as "the mother of all corn circles") that some researchers responded to the newspaper headline's challenge by 'explaining' it away as an 'obvious' hoax. As a knee-jerk reaction to a design that clearly failed to conform to any other conventional hypothesis, the reaction was understandable. Some people, however, were convinced that it was 'obviously' *not* a hoax, but seemed uncertain as to who or what caused it to appear, while others elected to exercise more caution by reserving judgement.

It was, after all, not the only event to occur in the surrounding area that night. Other occurrences included a circle at Wootton Bassett, an immaculate additional circle to the existing formation at Hackpen Hill, the enormous pictogram at Preshute Down, and an astonishing display of as yet unidentified luminosities observed from a point to the west of Beckhampton (of which I was a witness). It remains significant that most of those who were so prompt to label Barbury Castle a hoax revealed little or no sign of having investigated any of these other matters on a serious level. This remains so at the time of writing: not a shred of hard evidence has surfaced which enables us to validate the Barbury Castle pictogram as man-made.

The makers of the Barbury Castle formation had sculpted from the raw material of an ordinary cereal crop a highly sophisticated image which, alas, was destined to suffer a severe battering from the combined effects of human curiosity and inclement weather. As it happened, Barbury Castle remained in pristine condition for a lamentably short period of time, twenty-four hours at the most.

Reading the Cipher

To date, the number of researchers who have taken the trouble to consider the Barbury Castle pictogram as a designed construct are few. The notable exception was John Michell who, writing soon after the event occurred, remarked in an article of succinct authority that it contained "a world of symbolism . . . some of it already apparent and some still awaiting recognition"[2]. The purpose of this article is to explore not how the formation may have been created as such, but what, perhaps, it may signify in the light of its affinities in alchemy — for it is in alchemical lore that we recognise most, if not all, of its component parts. This, then, is an attempt to 'read' the symbol, and I must stress that the reading is both personal and speculative, without assuming in any way to be either correct or definitive. It is offered here in the genuine hope that it may encourage further analysis.

I'd like to start with the form of the 3-in-1 triangle; the apex of which was occupied by the central circle. This will be immediately recognisable to those familiar with the history of magical symbolism as a *Solomonic pentacle*, as used by both Pythagoreans and occultists, and known to have been employed in the casting of 'spells'. Inscribed around the circle perimeter in our example (fig a) is a quotation from Psalm XVIII-7, indicating that it was designed to invoke an earthquake. The use of such designs was founded in a belief in the divine properties of geometrical symbolism, by which practitioners of magical crafts sought to establish connections with supernatural forces. As emblems, pentacles were ineffective in themselves. Their primary function was to help focus the sensibilities of their users on the desired result.

The same triangular form also features prominently in alchemy, where it represents the triune Godhead or Trinity (fig b). It will be noted that in both of these illustrations the partitioned triangle is contained within another. How, then do they comply with the Barbury figure, where only the one triangle was found? Close study of

a. The 'Solomonic Pentacle' used by both the Pythagoreans and occultists in the casting of spells. The quotation from Psalm XVIII indicates it was designed to invoke an earthquake.

b. The Triune Godhead or Trinity.

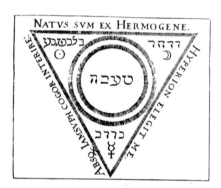

d. The *Silva Philosophorum of Cornelius Petraeus*, showing the divine operational pattern of the creative universe.

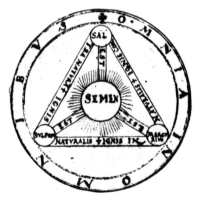

c. Circles enclosed by an equilateral triangle of the tenth key, attributed to Basil Valentine, 15th Century.

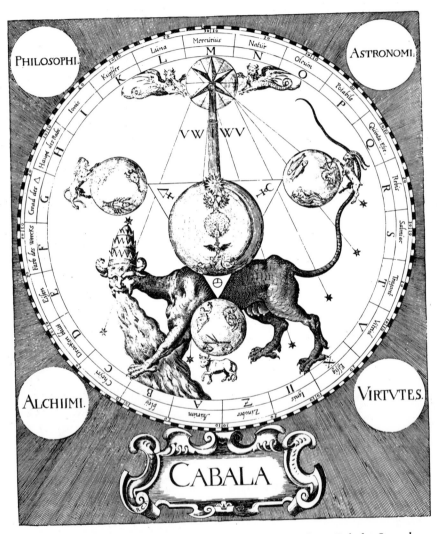

e. 'Exaltation', from a book by Steffan Michelspacher, *Cabala, Speculum Altis et Naturae in Alchymia*, published in 1654. A wheeling zodiac of good and bad signs encircling the composite image of the universal cow mother and evil dragon. See simplified version on back cover.

the figure demonstrates that the centre-points of the three outlying circular features form the points of an outer triangle which, although not etched in the corn, was an integral component of the overall design structure.

John Haddington has elsewhere[3] drawn attention to the depiction of a couple of circles enclosed by an equilateral triangle in a work attributed to Basil Valentine (fig c). Valentine was a legendary 15th century Benedictine monk whose actual existence has not been authenticated (since no original manuscripts have ever been found), but to whom was credited the invention of the theory of *Tria Prima*. This was a fundamental tenet of alchemy which proposed salt, sulphur and mercury as the three primary elements that underlie universal 'matter'. At its most reductive level, alchemy was said to be concerned with turning base metal into gold and anyone claiming knowledge of how to perform this miraculous feat was prone to personal danger from those who failed to appreciate its allegorical nature, by responding to the definition in a purely literal sense.

One of the principal reasons why alchemy fell into disrepute was its ruthless exploitation by charlatans who used it to make money out of those gullible enough to fall into their trap. This is portrayed in two masterpieces of English literature, Chaucer's *Canon's Yeoman's Tale* and Ben Johnson's *The Alchemist*. Sincere practitioners were more circumspect in their activities, sometimes expressing themselves through the agency of a fictitious character. It has been proposed that 'Basil Valentine' might well have been the adopted pseudonym of a Frankfurt salt-boiler by the name of Johann Tholde who worked on the books purported to have been written by Valentine at a time when German interest in the medical alchemy of Paracelsus was at its peak. Tholde had links with the Rosicrucian movement, which may have inspired him to invent an historic personage of uncertain birthright.

The Valentine texts once enjoyed a wide readership including Isaac Newton, who was fascinated by Valentine's survey of the properties of antimony. The most popular of Valentine's collections, *The Twelve Keys*, was first published in 1599 and reprinted in 1602. The first illustrated edition appeared in 1618 and was reprinted on numerous occasions during the 17th and 18th centuries. The twelve 'keys' represented the twelve stages of the alchemical process. The one that interests us here is the tenth.

The tenth key (fig **d**.), unlike the others in the sequence, was illustrated in diagrammatic form and was intended to designate 'the heavenly stone of the third conjunction', merging 'Sol and Luna in the trinitarian sign of Mercurius Philosophorum, or God'.

In simple terms, this was the alchemical 'Egg' or 'Stone' in the act of formation prior to the act of completion (ie 'creation' in the form of matter). At the centre of the circle is the name of the deity, with the symbols of the sun, moon and mercury at each point of the triangle.

The three inscriptions translate as follows: *I am born of Hermogenes* (the name refers to a Gnostic philosopher noted for the heretical assertion that 'God had created all things from co-existent and unregenerated matter'); *Hyperion elected me* (a reference to solar rebirth: in Greek mythology, Hyperion represented the god of the sun); and *without Jamsuph I am compelled to perish* (Jamsuph being an unknown substance or element by which the process of rebirth was sustained, and without which regeneration could not occur). Here, then, we find the three essential ingredients of alchemical philosophy (base material, reproduction, and that mysteriously-named component by which the material is transmuted, through reproduction, into another form) welded into a single image.

We turn next to the *Sylva Philosophorum* of Cornelius Petraeus, who described himself as a 16th century student of Hermetic philosophy from Hamburg. This work included eight cosmic diagrams, no less than six of which were of a shape which combined the features of Valentine's key with that of the three-in-one trinitarian triangle (fig d)[5]. Furthermore, each point of the triangle contains a circle. In this case, the symbol serves a multi-functional purpose by which the alchemical process of converting base metal into gold is perceived in transcendental terms. Our chosen example may show SEMEN as 'seed' of the 'Great Work', but the same cell-like structure is also employed to demonstrate GOD, MAN, NATURE, SOUL and the PHILOSOPHER'S STONE. The other two diagrams, of the Universe (*Quinta Essentia*) and the Four Elements, will be familiar to crop circle researchers for their uncanny resemblance to quintuplet formations. Through Petraeus, then, we learn that our symbol is intended to represent the divine operational pattern of the creative universe.

But how does alchemy relate to the Barbury cipher? An answer may be found in an illustration, depicting the Wheeling Zodiacal Circles of Exaltation, from a book by Steffan Michelspacher entitled *Cabala, Speculum Artis et Naturae, in Alchymia*, first published in Augsberg in 1654 (fig e). At last, we are confronted with an image which, though not an exact replication, corresponds closely to the

Barbury crop formation.

What is to be made of this daunting and striking design which, interestingly, was recently featured in a book on alchemy?[6] Starting with the unearthly beast, this fearsome creature, wearing a tiara on its horned head and spewing fire, has been interpreted by some as a representation of the Pope as Anti-Christ, but this is highly debatable. A more feasible view is that it is a composite image of the universal cow-mother/devil-dragon: the *Anima Mundi* (soul of the world). Also named *Adam Kadmon*, this is the hermaphroditic primordial being of the Qabala: the arcane substance, no less, or undifferentiated matter. Above it we find a triangle with an overlying circle in roughly the same position as the outer ring at Barbury Castle, and, at each point of the triangle, three other 'satellite' globes.

The tubular shaft extending northwards to the six-pointed star did not figure in the Barbury formation, for good reason: this is the 'celestial' star from which emanate six other stars — the one fixed on the tiara is representative of the same 'celestial' star, and its appropriate position is *above* the central circle, by which it is connected via the tube-like neck of the hermetic vessel. The extension is to be viewed in a three-dimensional sense, for the celestial star resides in the heavens above. It will also be observed that the wheel itself is surrounded by four other rings, forming the *Quinta Essentia* symbol (the universe), and that the signs of the zodiac are grouped together about the three satellite globes.

It is by means of this illustration that we establish a direct symbolic link between Barbury Castle and the Tree of Life of the Qabala. Space does not permit us to discuss this mystical belief system in depth, but what merits our attention is a certain likeness between the Barbury cipher and the relationships between the Lower Sephiroth on the Tree of Life, clearly inferred by the artist at the foot of the page. The Lower Sephiroth or 'circles' are the activating agents through which the Divine becomes Manifest in a relationship which, according to Qabalistic thought, permeates all living things and objects without exception.

The world of matter is energised by the grounding of a 'lightning flash' from above, and the flow of energy between the circles; creation being dependent on their operating together as one. Each globe or Sephira has a different complementary function: one serves as the point of energy 'transmission'; one as the reverberating 'repeater'; one as the 'absorber' (equivalent, in electrical terms, to the 'earth' function); and another, at the centre, as the point of stabilisation and convergence, balancing energies from the 'celestial star' above, which is only rendered visible to mankind as heavenly light (the celestial star being the point of contact between heaven and earth)[7].

If the above comes across as obscure, then the fault is entirely mine for trying to summarise something of renowned subtlety in as few words as possible. Nevertheless, the point is that, oddly enough, the crop marks at Barbury Castle *appear to conform symbolically with the functions I have just outlined*. The partially-pierced ring is equatable with the absorbent or 'earth' function; the so-called 'sun-wheel' with that of the repeater or radiator; the ratchet spiral with transmission. It may also be of interest to note that the 'lower' world of the Qabala is the world of shells and that the pattern was positioned on a groundbase of aquiferous chalk (as, indeed, are the majority of crop circles), a material composed of almost pure calcium carbonate and containing countless minute fossil fragments of ancient shelled marine creatures.

I would suggest at this point that with the antecedents detailed here, one may read the Barbury cipher as a graphic representation of the 'philosopher's stone' or 'cosmic egg' from which all life is derived, at the stage in the transmutation of matter which precedes the act of completion. The final stage is the *fall into creation*, and in order to make some sort of sense of the fall we should recall that in 'Exaltation' our design is enclosed in a rotating zodiacal wheel. The Great Work is completed by activating the wheel. Once in motion, the constituent elements are blended and once again, through rotation, rendered invisible.

Once transmutation has occurred, we are back at the beginning of the process. Form, having been broken down and reconstituted, yields its 'secret' in the moment that finds it ready to assume form again. In alchemy, this process is symbolised by a serpent/dragon, an Ouroboros, describing a circle to swallow its tail at the point where the beginning (Alpha) and end (Omega) conjoin. This is the point where the alchemist, in the words of W E Butler, discovers the "powers and forces which already exist and work in nature" [8]. The Barbury configuration was, then, a symbolic figure of the divine order that exists at the interface between one level of matter and another, with seemingly infinite potentials.

"One's rational mind shrinks away from the implication that this diagram constitutes a divine revelation . . ." said John Michell[9], and well said. The rational mind *does* shrink from the notion, and yet divine revelation is *precisely* what it signifies. But let us dispense with divinity for a moment and consider this: if the structure of the Barbury Castle formation affords us a symbolic glimpse of the interface between one level of matter and another, then we might argue that this 'divine revelation' has a rational equivalent in contemporary science. For the *Massas Confusa* of alchemical and Hermetic tradition, read *Chaos Theory*, and visualise the manner in which the Mandelbrot Set operates as a fractal image residing at the boundary between one level of reality and another, with similar transmutable qualities. Both patterns represent the nexus between chaos and order where one world contains all the potentials required to beget another.

I have deliberately resisted exploring the general geometric principles of the Barbury Castle formation for the simple reason that the topic warrants a detailed study of its own. The one detail that I would like to mention here, however, concerns the 'ratchet' feature in which the crop was flattened *outwards* from a small centre circle prior to meeting the point of the triangle. This was not only a difficult exercise to perform, but one which actually supports the idea of the ratchet as a point of transmission. Was the small centre circle of the ratchet the residual mark of a 'lightning strike' from above? It's an interesting proposition, certainly, and one which is unnervingly consistent with the symbolic meaning of the overall design.

This reading contends that *the Barbury Castle cipher can be interpreted as an alchemical version of the Mandelbrot Set*, both symbols existing as diagrammatic images of chaos and order. There is, of course, nothing particularly new about this in terms of 'revelation', as it is one which has been 'revealed' to mystics and sages in various ways throughout human history. The ancient Babylonians, for example, believed that 'chaos' had many faces, and we might argue that the Barbury Castle cipher represents a face possessing the potential to reveal countless, if not all, other faces.

As such, the image also represents the Triune Godhead and qualifies to be described as the mother, father and offspring of all crop circles. The quality which renders this possible, the alchemical secret of life, is known by a multitude of names, but in essence is the Unnameable and Unutterable Word of God. This Word can be alluded to in an infinite variety of ways, and what was carved into the corn at Barbury Castle was nothing short of a mannered expression of the Absolute made manifest.

A Postscript on hoaxing

Reading the image does not, of course, necessarily explain how it materialised in a cornfield during the night of July 16th/17th 1991, and yet it does appear to hint at a possible cause: that of a divine, or, if you like, supernatural agency which operated through a 'lightning strike'. Does the symbol itself reveal the secret of its origin? Or did persons as yet unknown deliberately strive to cultivate such a response by creating this particular impression at Barbury Castle?

Elsewhere in this book, Beth Davis and George Wingfield report on the Mandelbrot Set at Ickleton, near Cambridge. Was it mere chance that not one but two complex graphic images of transmutation, one archaic and the other modern, appeared in the fields within weeks of one another? Is it reasonable to consider them hoaxed by different groups who were completely unaware of the symbolic compatibility of their chosen designs? I doubt it. Then again, they could have been created by the *same* group. But for what purpose? To literally 'draw' the connection outlined here as some sort of corny cosmic prank? If so, their efforts displayed an acute conceptual intelligence: that of an anonymous Magus-like architect, maybe? At least a few of those currently investigating the hoax hypothesis tend to think so, and the involvement of an individual or group of persons well-versed in magical rites and sacred geometry is strongly suspected. If something of the kind transpires to be true, then hoaxing on such a scale has to be regarded as graffiti art of an increasingly impressive quality. Any number of groups may be involved, perhaps in competition with one another. In which case, we can expect the stakes to be rising all the time as one group labours to establish its ascendancy over its peers by producing ever-more fantastic shapes.

In my view, those who created the Barbury cipher were probably way ahead of everyone else, for a few weeks at least. But is this straining our credibility just a little too far? There are a number of additional problems regarding the night on which it appeared, that might possibly have some bearing on the matter, and Gary Hardwick's account of the luminosities contains a potentially pertinent detail about which, in conclusion, I would like to add a few words.

Of particular interest here was the thin white beam which all three of us saw curving towards the ground. Visible for no longer than a couple of seconds, after which its apparent luminosity began to dissipate before our eyes, the beam conspicuously failed to illuminate any part of the surrounding sky and appeared entirely self-contained. The beam incident occurred at approximately 1am, and ground contact was established due north of our location at the Needles' Point lay-by. On returning home that night, I consulted various maps and estimated that the beam must have touched earth somewhere between Clyffe Pypard and Wootton Bassett.

What I did not know then, of course, was that a crop circle appeared during the course of that night at Wootton Bassett. This circle has been suspected by some of having been hoaxed, and yet, because of the beam, I doubt that. There is no evidence to prove that the beam of light was in any way involved in the appearance of that particular circle, but the coincidence of two apparently anomalous events seems to me as suspicious as any other proposition. Although not perceived as hollow, this light beam may have been similar in some respects to that seen by Mary Freeman at Avebury in July 1988, and my attempts to read the Barbury cipher have given me cause to wonder whether the 'lightning strike' to which I have earlier referred might involve an emission such as that witnessed by Gary, Alison and myself.

This gives rise to the intriguing possibility that, two or three hours later, something of the same kind also made contact with the ground at Barbury Castle. This is mere conjecture, of course, and cannot be affirmed. If it did, then the symbol might have been drawn by an aerial entity as unfamiliar as that which emitted a beam of light to the ground somewhere in the vicinity of Wootton Bassett.

The Warden of Barbury Castle was disturbed from his sleep at approximately 3am by a loud roaring noise, and an entire flock of sheep was terrified into deserting the slope under which the cipher appeared — they were found scattered over the opposite side of the hill around 7-8am. It is interesting to note that a similar case of frightened sheep occurred only a few days later at Lapworth, Warwickshire, during the night of July 19th, when a single circle was formed in a nearby field.

I suspect that something of an extraordinary nature took place at

Barbury Castle during the night in question. Whether or not it was linked to any of the other anomalous events that occurred in the local environment I cannot say for sure, but of this I am certain: that the night of July 16th/17th merits a good deal more attention than it has received to date and, as this report has sought to demonstrate, the Barbury Castle cipher is by no means easy to explain away: those who were so quick to declare it a hoax did so without researching the case as diligently as the design deserved.

NOTES

1. *Western Daily Press*, Thursday, July 18, 1991.
2. Michell, John: 'Geometry and Symbolism at Barbury Castle', in *The Cerealogist*, No 4, Summer 1991, pp24-25.
3. *Global Link-Up*, No. 49, October/November 1991.
4. Fabricius, J.: *Alchemy*, Aquarian Press, London, 1989, p165, for an excellent and thought-provoking translation of Valentine's commentary to the tenth key. "When you have dissolved your earth with your water, dry up the water with its own proper fire. Then the air will breathe new life, and when this has again turned into a body, then you will have that matter which nobody else can have. For the great stone of the world which in a spiritual manner pervades human and metallic bodies is the universal and immaculate medicine, since it drives out that which is bad and preserves that which is good, and is the unfailing corrective of all imperfect or diseased substances . . . whoever gained possession of this stone should thank the Supreme Creator of all creatures for such a heavenly balm."
5. De Rola, Stanislas Klossowski: *Alchemy: The Secret Art*, Thames & Hudson, London, 1973, pp120-122, for the full set of eight cosmic diagrams and the original title page, with its quotation from Deuteronomy XXXIII: 13-16, which begins: "*Blessed of the Lord be his land, for the precious things of heaven, for the dew, and for the deep that croucheth beneath . . .* ". The latter phrase is interesting in that the 'deep' in Barbury's case was aquiferous chalk, its 'earth' being both solid and watery.
6. Fabricius, J: *ibid*, p53.
7. Halevi, Z'ev ben Shimon: *The Tree of Life*, Rider, 1972, reprinted by Gateway Books, 1991, for a useful and highly lucid introduction to the Qabala.
8. Butler, W E: *Lords of Light*, Destiny Books, 1990, p102.
9. Michell, John: *ibid*.

Pulsing Lights at Beckhampton

Gary Hardwick

This is a report of a series of pulsing lights that were observed in the sky above Wiltshire on the night of 16th-17th July 1991. I can offer no explanation of what happened on that night. What follows is a description only of what I observed.

At about 11.50pm, on the A4 just west of Beckhampton round-about, near Avebury, I was in a car driven by my girlfriend Alison, and we also had with us Brian Grist in the rear off-side passenger seat. At that moment, Brian shouted that we should stop and pull over, and Alison drove into a lay-by which could just be glimpsed in the headlights. Brian had seen a pulsing light through the near-side window. The light was of a green hue and seemed immediately to be unusual. It was larger than the surrounding stars and was strangely solitary.

Brian and I leapt out of the car — or rather Brian did and I followed — and Alison remained in the car, not quite sure of what we were up to. We stood outside and watched as this light pulsed green and red to the left of the lay-by, towards the south of the road. It was travelling in a westerly direction towards Calne. There was no noise. Alison got out and joined us, and we stood for a few minutes in the cold, watching it track slowly across the sky. Suddenly the lay-by lit up and a car pulled away from the far end, and passed us.

I had a pair of field glasses which I attempted to focus on the light. I handed them to Brian. I then noticed another light moving behind us, over the other side of the A4, moving in the same direction — westwards. I pointed out this light to Brian, and at that moment started to feel a little confused, as I had not previously witnessed anything quite like this before. For some reason I looked straight above where I was standing — vertically into the night sky, which was clear and peppered with stars. In an instant, probably no more than two or three seconds, I saw above me a black shape, narrow at the front and wide at the rear, which obscured the stars and which passed eastward at incredible speed and totally silently towards the horizon. This happened so quickly that I would normally have dismissed it. I could not believe that Alison had seen the same as I had. To this day, if it had not been for her corroboration I would not have believed it. I have since questioned her at length and thought hard myself about that moment. She remains adamant that what she saw was the same as I have described.

I have attempted to give it a shape, and all that I can say is that it resembled a triangle. It was quite high up and was large enough for me to notice that it obscured quite a significant portion of the sky. Its brief path over our heads seemed effortless. It moved with such haste that it is unlikely that anyone would have been aware of it, had they not looked into a clear sky at that precise moment. Indeed Brian was not aware of it. I was left with an overwhelming feeling of having seen something so powerful that any attempt at decoding its possible meaning would be futile. I have a feeling that the path it chose was the safest, being directly above our heads, when we were all watching the horizon.

Light Number One had by now gone, and Light Two had stopped moving to the naked eye and was just sitting in the sky in the general direction of Windmill Hill. Through the field glasses it could be seen pulsing white, green, and green-blue; it had no discernible shape.

We next became aware of Lights Three and Four across the road towards the north. These seemed to be much further away, and were moving in downward curves towards each other. From our viewpoint it seemed as though they would collide. They were pulsing like the uncoordinated flashing of the two lights on the roof of an emergency vehicle, like an ambulance — in sequence, and then slowly out of sequence again. They passed each other, and continued on their downward arcs and disappeared below the horizon.

We felt that it was time to go, and that we had seen quite enough. It was by this time getting *very* cold. We returned to the car and were about to rejoin the main A4, when Brian again shouted that we should stop. We all got out of the car, with the engine still running and the lights still on. What Brian had seen, and we now all saw together, was a much larger light of pulsing red in vertical motion. It was again to the north of the A4 and was moving slowly westwards. Its movement also seemed quite jerky, which could be to do with its distance from us. However, it also seemed to be quite large in comparison to the earlier lights. I had to steady the field glasses on the roof of the car and hold my breath. Having done this, what I saw was a column of red, green and white pulses, alternating direction from bottom to top and vice versa.

We became aware of Light Six as Light Five was still moving in a westerly direction. It was moving from the north to the south, and across the road to our east. It also seemed to move relatively slowly, and then suddenly quicken, and just as suddenly slow down again. This could of course be due to distance: the night air could refract the light source and make it appear jerky. However, this would have to mean that it was very large indeed, much bigger than Lights One to Four.

On looking through the field glasses, I observed that it was pulsing backwards and forwards in hues of green, pink, white and blue, but on a horizontal plane. It, like Light Five, had more shape — its predecessors being a mixture of pulsing hues. This again made me wonder whether it was either much closer or much larger.

Light Five, the vertical column, was by now very low in the sky. Suddenly we saw a very thin white beam of light join it to the ground. This beam was curved, not straight or jagged, and lasted one to two seconds. Light Five then disappeared, or rather faded, quite quickly.

At this time, Light Six was fading towards the south, and we all agreed to go home. We had been watching the events for about one hour. It was almost one o'clock on the morning of July 17th. Light Number Two remained stationary, and in view through the window of the car until we reached Calne, when the lights of the town submerged it. We all remained silent until we reached Bristol.

At no time in the hour-long observation did any of us hear a noise. In fact we remarked that the night was totally silent, apart from the sound of the occasional car on the A4. We all believed that what we had seen had not behaved like six conventional aircraft. I am not aware of anything that can move to a position in the sky, and stay motionless without emitting any engine noise.

The place where we stopped the car on the night of 16th-17th is called Needles Point. We did not know that we had stopped there initially — it was very dark and our decision to stop was sudden. It was however the same spot that Brian Grist and I stopped at in Summer 1990, on one bright morning, and saw through field-glasses the two 'scrolls' and the triangle crop formation, in a field farmed by Steven Horton. It turned out that we were among the first people to go into the field and examine the formation on that occasion.

On 17th July 1991, the morning after the events I have described, the formation at Barbury Castle was discovered. That particular pattern is the subject of another chapter, but I will conclude with some comments concerning a meeting that Brian, Alison and I had with the warden of Barbury Castle, about a week later. The gentleman concerned lives in a bungalow on the east side of Barbury Castle, where he has a shop in the summer months, selling refreshments to people out walking. He also farms sheep that graze the slopes surrounding the earth-works. We asked him about the night of 16th-17th July, and he said that he was awakened at about 3am by what he described as 'a low throbbing sound' in the sky above. He said that it sounded like a hundred aircraft in formation, passing overhead. The next morning he went looking for his two flocks as usual. One is normally penned to the south, and the other one shelters beneath the north slope. He found that the flock that shelters on the northern slope had scattered, and were found towards the south. They would have to have gone up a steep hill and across the ramparts, and the warden concluded that they must have been very frightened to do this. They could have been disturbed by the same noise that had woken him. We attempted to find out how long he thought the noise had lasted, but he was unable to remember. However, he did say that the noise 'suddenly stopped'.

The warden was not aware of the Barbury Castle formation until, when tending his sheep, he was stopped by a group of German tourists, who wanted to know where the crop circle was. This was about noon on 17th July.

The Serpent at Froxfield

Jürgen Krönig

The first time I saw the 'Serpent' or 'Brain', it was only a dark, shadowy spot on the golden carpet of an over-ripe wheat field near Froxfield, just a mile from the border of Berkshire and Wiltshire. In fact, it was Nick Bailey who was the first to spot this extraordinary formation. Nick was the pilot of a small two-seater helicopter, with whom I had flown many times during the summer of 1991.

We were just at the end of a flight over parts of North Wiltshire, and Nick circled the helicopter over the huge 'dolphin' formation near Froxfield. Out of the corner of his eye, he had spotted a dark marking in a field approximately three-quarters of a mile away, while I was busy photographing the 'dolphin'. We decided to have a closer look and flew over the fields and woodlands.

When we arrived we were both stunned. Never before had we seen anything like this: a free-flowing form of passageways, evolving from small circles, some of them running precisely on a parallel course to each other. We hovered above the formation for a time, while I took a lot of photographs. We were both fascinated by this completely new and exciting pictogram. Nick brought the helicopter down to a height of not more than 15-20 feet, just high enough not to damage the fragile structure of the pictogram, but low enough to see how completely untouched this crop formation looked.

We couldn't detect any marks or footprints in the surrounding fields, but discovered another small circle just at the edge of the field. We then flew along the edges of the wheat-field to look for anything unusual. All we found was another pair of circles, half a mile away, just beside a small country lane. The bigger of these circles just touched the edge of the field in which, two days later, another pictogram appeared in the shape of a turtle, an oval 'body' with four short 'legs'.

Approximately one hour later I was back at the scene. Having returned from the flight, I asked my wife Katharina and a friend from

Germany, Rainer Traube, to join me and have a closer look at the new pictogram near Froxfield. I had marked the location on an Ordnance Survey map, so knew where we had to go to look for it. Nevertheless, it proved difficult to find. Whoever was responsible for this formation, had obviously not intended it to be a showpiece for the wider public. A wise decision perhaps, because its fragile structure would not have withstood hundreds of trampling feet as easily as some of the more accessible circles.

We parked the car on an earth track at the edge of a woodland, but were not able to find an obvious entrance to the wheat-field which contained the circle. Nor was it possible, looking over the field, to see any indication that, somewhere, there was a labyrinth of curved pathways. We walked along the side of the wheat field, and then spotted the small circle at the edge of it. The circle was not connected to any of the tram-lines. We walked carefully through the surrounding corn, trying to cause as little damage as possible.

The circle had all of the features that are so well-known by now, and are regarded to be the hallmark of the 'genuine article'. The swirled centre was slightly off-centre, and the stems of corn were not

The flow starts again after an abrupt interruption. (Jürgen Krönig).

broken. I moved out of the circle along one of the tram-lines, which ran unusually far apart from one another. The farmer obviously uses very large spraying machinery. The tram-lines were overgrown with secondary growth. No foot had trodden them for quite a while. Walking further into the field, I suddenly saw something that looked like wind damage. Then at last I realised that we had found the pattern we had been looking for. I gave a sign to Katharina and Rainer, who had stayed behind in the small circle.

Together we entered the first circle from which the network of pathways emerged. We were impressed by the complexity and accuracy. We noticed that the pathways sometimes ended abruptly, just a few inches before reaching a tram-line, leaving only a thin row of standing wheat. There were no indications that anybody had entered this pictogram before. Everything seemed completely untouched. Parts of the network of pathways were lying totally separated from tram-lines. We checked to see if somebody, however carefully, had managed to enter these pathways by walking through the surrounding crop — we were unable to detect even the slightest indication of human entry. Not one stem of wheat was even slightly out of place. We decided not to enter the inaccessible parts of the pictogram.

Slowly we managed to explore the whole formation. We noticed that some of the wheat-stems in the pathways were still standing: it looked as if they had been cut off at a height of approximately 22 inches, and the surface of the cut was blackened. All three of us agreed that this was not only one of the most remarkable formations we had seen, but also we were certain that it was virtually impossible to imagine even an extremely sophisticated ground-based hoaxer could have done this. All tram-lines were considerably overgrown, some of the circles and a few of the pathways were inaccessible, and in some places the bent wheat-stems of the pathways were 'flowing' around single, completely untouched stems.

We spent nearly two hours in this formation. The daylight was fading. Sitting in the largest of the circles we discussed our impressions and observations. What did it resemble most? Was it a symbol? And if so, what was the meaning? The name that sprang to my mind was '*brain*'. Maybe '*serpent*' is also an adequate, if not a better name. On the other hand, *if* the circles are directed at our human consciousness, '*brain*' doesn't seem too far off the mark.

The following day, Katharina and I returned to the 'Brain'. We had

One of the small circles appears to have been 'brushed'. (Jürgen Krönig).

invited Pat Delgado to come along and inspect this extraordinary formation. Pat, who certainly has seen many beautiful circles before, was impressed. He too noticed the strange black marks on some of the wheat-stems, and collected a few samples. Two young men and two students from Germany, who had discovered the formation while flying a microlite, had arrived shortly before we did. It was interesting to notice that these visitors too had decided not to enter the inaccessible parts of the formation, for fear of damaging it. Only very few people had a chance to see this amazing pictogram. The field was harvested four days after we had had the luck to discover the 'brain'.

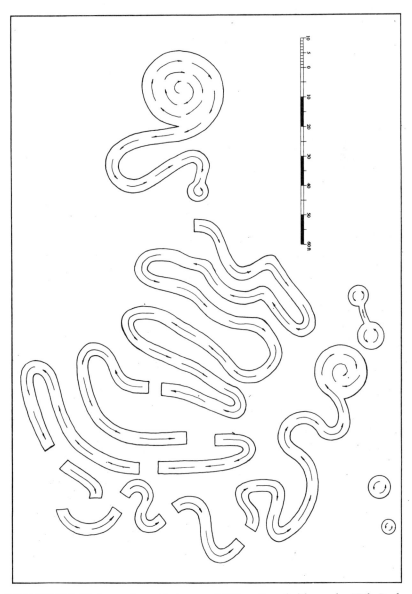

THE SERPENT, formed on 18 August 1991 at Froxfield, on the Wilt-Berks border. (J.F. Langrish drawing).

The Serpent: A Genetic Analogy

Beth Davis

"We are living in what the Greeks called the Kaitos — *the right time — for a 'metamorphosis of the Gods', . . . This peculiarity of our time, which is certainly not of our conscious choosing, is the expression of the unconscious man within us who is changing."*

Carl Jung, 1958.

Two Mayan stone tablets have just recently been decoded by archaeologists in Texas, USA. They describe the genesis of the Mayan world as it was understood more than 2,000 years ago. The world was at first a two-dimensional world of land and sky, transformed by a natural force — the primordial flame of creation, through the action of the Milky Way. They believed that the Milky Way was used as a great tree which supported the sky and gave the Earth its three-dimensional form.

Scientists, without knowing the raw chemicals of our planet before life began, have made comparisons with other planets in our solar system and found four common compounds, water, carbon dioxide, methane and ammonia. Also with traces of hydrogen, a famous laboratory experiment was carried out in 1953 at the University of Chicago[1] to simulate the primordial conditions that could have existed. By applying an electro-magnetic charge imitating lightning repeatedly for several days, a brown soup — the 'primordial soup' — was formed. It included in the mix the complex molecules necessary for life on Earth. Ultra-violet light was substituted for the electro-magnetic charge, with similar results. However, as life on earth has evolved, an oxygen-rich atmosphere has resulted, shielding the ultra-violet light, which had become life-threatening to the developing forms of life.

Two of these organic substances from the primordial soup are contained in the molecule DNA which is present in every living cell of plants, animals, bacteria and viruses[2]. The DNA molecule holds the code for self-replication — that is, it is able to make an exact copy of itself and the cell it encodes.

Occasionally there are minor alterations in this self-replicating process, which causes the cell to change its original form. This may be beneficial, or non-beneficial to the living organism, and by this process and through 'natural selection' the living organism evolves. Darwin's theory of evolution by natural selection was published years after his original discoveries, and when he did publish it, it revolutionised scientific thought and research.

One hundred years later, in 1953, at Cambridge University, two brilliant young scientists, James Watson and Francis Crick, discovered the message of our inheritance, and of every living thing on earth, written in the spirals of the double helix molecule of DNA. Their epic story in the race to be first with this remarkable information is retold in *The Double Helix* by Watson[3]. In 1962 Watson and Crick were awarded the Nobel Prize for this discovery, believed to be the greatest scientific discovery of this century.

The DNA molecule is composed of two strands which are spiralled together in a double helix[4]. Each strand is made up of a genetic 'alphabet', the order of which is specific to that molecule. Each 'letter' of the alphabet pairs with the appropriate 'letter' on the other strand.

How does this genetic information relate to this curious formation of circles connected and disconnected by a wiggly line at Froxfield? The closest resemblance to any known shape like this is to a chromosome, seen under a microscope; this was a comment made to Alick Bartholomew by a friend who was a brain surgeon. The chromosome appears like this in the cell of a living organism at a specific time when it is about to divide to renew itself, or to reproduce itself as self-replicating individual cells. This can be seen in the diagrams showing this change, which is called *mitosis*, and *meiosis*[5].

Each living cell contains a nucleus, with its chromosomes. In man there are 23 pairs of chromosomes. Each chromosome is made up of strings of genes, each uniquely identified by its DNA sequence, and carrying the genetic code for every part of the body. There are uncoded areas on the DNA which are believed to be the receivers of signals of information. The DNA code is identical in each living cell, carrying information for the heart cells, the brain, the toe and so on: yet how does each cell know how to create and recreate itself in its own specialised way other than by receiving specific information?

The life of the chromosome in the nucleus is unique to the life of its living organism. It contains past information from an infinite branching line of ancestors, and it survives by means of inheritance — by the birth of a child, for example, who receives a genetic code with one set of chromosomes from each parent at the time of fertilisation. There is a potential for DNA to survive for thousands, and perhaps millions of years: it *has* already survived for eons!

Philosophers and scientists have always been aware of another essential component of life, "*Matter of itself has no power to do, to make, or to become: it is in energy that all these potentialities reside, energy invisibly associated with the material system, and in interaction with the energies of the surrounding universe*" — D'Arcy Thompson.[5] The Greeks postulated the existence of life-giving tension 'tones' which supported and moved all things. Carl Jung, philosopher and psychoanalyst, in his writings on inherited characteristics, said that we inherit a genetic structure with a program on how it should be used, but also with something apart from this. In a wider context, we are able, as a species, to adapt unconsciously to the physical conditions of the world in which we live, and at the same time to share inherited patterns of our past. The mechanism for this he termed the *collective unconscious*[6]. When actions and thought occur spontaneously to separate individuals, at apparently the same time, he called this *synchronicity*. This is the unseen connection we have with individuals and groups of our own species. Rupert Sheldrake explores and develops these ideas in the realms of natural behaviour. In his book *The Presence of the Past*[7], he recognises this *non-material organising principle* as part of our being, which also surrounds and envelopes us. His term for this is *morphic resonance*; it is not fixed, though its influence does not decline in time or space, but evolves with the system it organises[7].

It would appear that every living thing is unconsciously acting as a receiver in the living world, of the past and the present, and perhaps the future, where the mechanics of time and space may not be relevant. This is perhaps what the indigenous people are aware of. John and Julie Wakefield discuss this in the next article.

Today the medical bookshelves carry numerous copies of books on genetics. It is an expanding field of medical research which can be beneficial to all forms of life. *Genetic engineering* is frequently the term used where alterations are artificially made to the arrangement of chromosomes in a living cell. By a careful study of human genes,

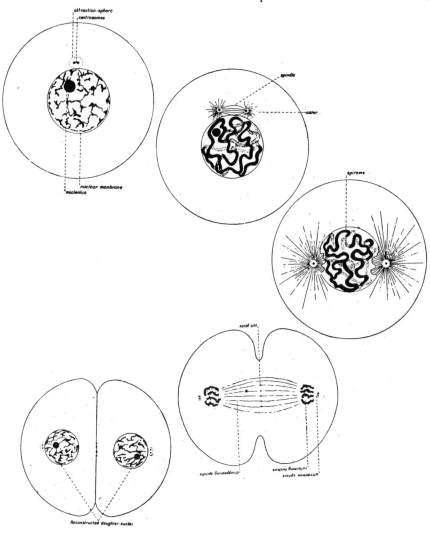

CELL DIVISION. Cells may differ in their structure, but share many common features. The *nucleus* within the cell contains the chromosomes, suspended in *nucleoplasm*. New cells are formed by the division of the original parent cell into two daughter cells. The exact duplication of the chromosomes occurs before cell division, when each chromosome splits to form two identical chromosomes, which migrate to the two *centronomes*. The membrane of the cell is pinched in two by constriction, and divides. This form of cell division is called *mitosis*. In reprduction, a cell will only contain half the chromosome numbers — the other half, at the time of fertilisation, restores the cell to the full number. This transformation is called *meiosis*.

more than 4,000 diseases are now known to arise from genetic defects. James Watson has spearheaded The Human Genome Project, from Cold Spring Harbor Laboratory, Long Island, New York. Envisaged as an international project, the US is clearly leading the way. His concern expressed recently is that *"as more and more things are revealed to have genetic components, we may see a feeling of losing control over our own destiny ... I don't believe that a lessening of respect for human life will occur, but we should be aware of commercial interests in this field"*.[8] Genetic mapping has also revealed the origins of certain groups of people, for example the Basques, who are still identified as a unique group, and the Etruscans in central Italy, whose descendants remain in the area even though their language and culture disappeared in classical times.

Jürgen Krönig noticed that the Froxfield crop formation was distinctly fragmented. This was perhaps by careful design for it would have been far simpler to have continued the wriggling path. It could be seen to be an imitation of a chromosome under the microscope, where part of the chromosome strand is out of focus; on the other hand it could be a chromosome aberration which appears as one or several breaks in the strand. This is the more likely as the break at each fragmented piece of the formation was very abrupt. Chromosome breakage is known to increase by exposure to ionising radiation, that is, ultra-violet radiation, which is directly controlled by the natural shield of the earth's ozone layer. The fractures in the chromosome are able to heal, but their rearrangement and subsequent character can be altered when this occurs naturally.

If there is indeed a meaning in this formation, perhaps it is demonstrating to all living things the danger that they may be exposed to by all man's *engineering*. It is more than a coincidence that the crop circles appear mostly in the northern hemisphere, and in one of the areas of greatest risk from ozone depletion in the atmosphere we should not be so complacent and should heed the warning by Carl Jung *"if humanity is not to destroy itself* (by) *the might of its own technology and science"*.

NOTES

1. Russell, Peter, *The Awakening Earth — Our Next Evolutionary Leap*, Routledge & Kegan Paul, London, 1982, p29.

2. Davies, Paul, *Superforce — The Search for a Grand Unified Theory of Nature*, Unwin, London, 1985.
3. Watson, James D, *The Double Helix*, Penguin, Harmondsworth, 1967.
4. Connor, J M, and Ferguson-Smith, M A, *Essential Medical Genetics*, Blackwell Scientific Publications, Oxford, 1991.
5. Thompson, D'Arcy W, *Growth and Form*, Cambridge University Press, 1942, pp304–309. Also: Connor, J M, *ibid*.
6. Jung, Carl, *Man and his Symbols*, Aldous/Jupiter, London, 1964, pp306–307.
7. Sheldrake, Rupert, *The Presence of the Past*,
8. Wilkie, Tom, *Leonardo, the Age of Discoveries*, The Independent, London, 1992, p78.
9. Connor, J M, *ibid*, p60.
10. Schneider, Stephen H, *Global Warming*, Lutterworth, Cambridge, 1989.
11. Jung, Carl, *The Undiscovered Self*, Routledge & Kegan Paul, 1958.
12. *The Cerealogist*, no.6, 1992. Michael Carost "What happened to the 'Radionuclides Paper'?". Plant DNA samples from inside the Argonne circle (USA) were considerably more degraded than DNA from outside it.

The Transformation of DNA

John and Julie Wakefield

Many crop circles are approximate replicas of symbols that were sacred to our ancestors. The circle itself is symbolic of oneness and cosmic consciousness. The Sioux holy man Black Elk, born in 1863, said that the circle is peace. Everything we do is done in a circle. It represents harmony. The universe consists of many circles that fit into larger circles, and each circle is connected. The power of the universe is contained within the circle. Each family is a circle and these connect to form a community circle. Everyone in the circle is to be looked after and respected. The circle is equality. The circle is holy. Everything is related in the circle of life. With this in mind we should in turn be humble.[1]

Crop circles are undoubtedly one of the biggest mysteries of the twentieth century. They pose puzzling questions to our rational way of thinking, and undermine our mechanistic view of nature. But many answers we seek from crop circles can be found in the ancient prophecies of indigenous peoples. Native Americans are at present choosing to speak out in order to help us in the West, by revealing many of their ancient teachings, secret traditions and prophecies. They feel it is important to do this, because they say something very serious is happening to the earth, and we need to understand what that is. So what do they believe is happening? What is their understanding of the crop circles? And where do we fit into all of this?

Native Americans say we are entering a new epoch, which their ancestors have foretold. The Hopi of Arizona, for example, state that we are moving into a 'fifth world', and their prophecies have been designed to guide us through this transition. In 1986, a council of indigenous peoples from all over South America held a Gathering of the Confederation of Tiwantinsuyo, in Machu Picchu, Peru, where it was decided that they would begin to re-open the ancient Mayan centres. In August 1987, a major event took place, when elders and shamans from remote parts of the world joined together to re-open and re-activate ancient sacred sites on a global scale, in order to aid our entrance into the new epoch.

Ceremonies have been held each year since and in 1989 the elders decided to join together again to reactivate a Mayan centre known as Chichēn Itzā, the purpose being to reprogram our DNA so that we can successfully adjust to the evolutionary changes now required of us. Hunbatz Men, author of *Secrets of Mayan Science and Religion*[2], and a Mayan Daykeeper (an authority on the history, calendars, chronology and knowledge of the Maya civilisation) was one of the elders present at this important event. He states that our DNA developed a major flaw which allowed humanity to develop individual ego. In order to reconnect with Nature and the divine, this defect must be changed.[3]. We can eradicate this flaw by altering the frequency of our minds, because all matter is vibration. He says that within our DNA is contained the wisdom our ancestors held. Dhyani Ywahoo, an Etowah Cherokee chieftainess, shares the same view, and states: "Wisdom is within the very fibres of our DNA structure. Wisdom already exists, and it is obscured only by mistakes in thinking"[4].

According to this, we must alter the frequency of our brain waves in order to change our thinking and to bring forward this vital wisdom in our DNA. But how can this be achieved?

Indigenous people believe that sacred centres such as stone circles — what they look on as *medicine wheels* — tumuli and pyramids were designed to cause different vibrations, which could alter the frequency of our brain waves. The ancient Maya, for example, foretold that the sacred sites would have to be reconsecrated, in order to help us strengthen our energy-bodies as we enter the new era. The elders say that during the transition to the new epoch, which began in 1987, and will be complete by 2013[5], the energy frequencies will be increasing, and it will be difficult for our bodies to cope. They say it is imperative that we make pilgrimages to our sacred centres, to re-open them, and ourselves.

Dr Eunice Baumann Nelson, a Penobscot Indian, says: "Given the fact that all people have within them the pre-natal memory of connectedness, there is the potential that this memory can be retrieved"[5]. The symbolism of crop formations is undoubtedly challenging, and leading to a raising of our consciousness, and in so doing, are helping us to retrieve this deep memory contained within our DNA.

So where do the crop circles come into all this? It has been clear for several years that the crop circles tend to cluster around our ancient sacred sites. There have been more crop formations in the 'Wessex Triangle' in southern England, with its proliferation of ancient sites such as Stonehenge and the Avebury complex, than anywhere else in the world. Why they should be appearing more in England than in other countries is still a mystery. The ancient Maya predicted that a time would come when the sacred symbols would be 'newly understood', and that this would herald an awakening for humanity. Is there a connection between these sacred symbols and the crop formations?

Ancient prophecies from many cultures, including Oriental ones, predict that the new epoch will not only bring a massive change in consciousness, but that it will also be a time of 'great purification'. This, they say, has already begun with earthquakes, volcanic eruptions, changes in weather and seasons of a different degree of change in our own time, and new threatening viruses. "We have teachings and prophecies informing us that we must be alert for the signs and omens which will come about. Nature will speak to us with its quakes and floods, causing great disasters". So said Hopi Elder Dan Katchongva, in 1970[7].

This is why the Indians are speaking out at this time. They say that it is vital that we recognise this need to change our DNA, so that we may survive this 'purification'. The dolphin-type formations in Wiltshire were found to contain levels of radiation which may be an example of the new energies and frequencies which will affect our DNA structure. It is more than just coincidence that the recent tests undertaken in British and American laboratories have demonstrated that the DNA structure of plants within crop formations has been altered. One biologist and a number of doctors have noted that the 'Serpent' or 'Brain' formation which appeared at Froxfield, Hungerford, in August 1991, resembles the appearance of a chromosome already described by Beth Davis. John Haddington also noted that the 'Double-headed Snail' formation of 1991, near Popham airfield, resembled the double helix structure of DNA.

There seemed to be a synchronicity in 1990 between the re-opening of the Mayan sacred sites and the dramatic change in the crop circle phenomenon in Britain when we witnessed the first pictograms. To us, there can be no doubt that there is a connection between what native people say is happening to human DNA, and what is happening to the plant-life in our crop fields.

NOTES

1. Neihardt, John, *Black Elk Speaks*, Univ Nebraska Press. Reprinted Bison Books, 1985.
2. Men, Hunbatz, *Secrets of Mayan Science and Religion*, Bear & Co, 1990. Hunbatz Men is the spokesperson for the South American Elders present at the various ceremonies which have been held these last few years, and is founder of the Mayan Indigenous Community. He is one of a few Indians who have had books and works published. It is difficult to obtain quotes from individual Indians, because shamans prefer to use a select few to speak for them collectively, so as not to reveal themselves on a personal basis. In the books already published there is a correlation of prophecies, dates and information from many different cultures, and all agree with the gist of this article. The prophecies of some tribes predicted that there would be a massive change in human consciousness, rather than using the term DNA, but in their eyes it means the same thing.
3. McFadden, Steven, ed, *Profiles in Wisdom*, Bear & Co, 1991, p235.
4. McFadden, Steven, ed, ibid., p55.
5. McFadden, Steven, ed, ibid., p227. Indians who have chosen to reveal and compare prophecies of their ancestors agree that we shall have fully entered the new era by 2011-13. Oh Shinnah says the Great Purification will be over by 2011, marked by the appearance of a new star. An Inca says we began to enter the new era in 1987, and will have made the transition by 2013, when the ancient calendars end. Hunbatz Men says we will have fully entered the new era by 2013, and that if we see large white circles in the sky, it will mean we will have failed to make a successful transition.
6. McFadden, Steven, ed, ibid., p79.
7. Boissiere, Robert, *The Return of the Pahana*, Bear & Co, 1990, p28.

Ciphers in a Time of Change

Jürgen Krönig

Looking at these three remarkable ciphers which we chose to study thoroughly, it becomes obvious that they represent symbols of great importance. It is difficult to resist the conclusion that the circle-makers chose these symbols on purpose. All of them are not only strikingly beautiful: all of them represent, or seem to represent, a link between human consciousness and the surrounding world.

Barbury Castle is a symbol of sacred geometry. As John Michell points out, "it demonstrates the principle of three-in-one, by means of a central circle that contains the combined areas of the three circles around it"[1]. Brian Grist discovered that it resembles one of the most important symbols of alchemy — again, three-in-one. The Mandelbrot fractal is the best and most widely-known graph of a new mathematical theory which expresses the implicate order behind a seemingly chaotic universe. The similarity between the free-flowing 'Serpent' or 'Brain' and a DNA chromosome is more than a coincidence, a synchronicity laid out in a cornfield.

Whether or not one is prepared to share the conclusions presented in this book, the question remains to be answered: what form of intelligence is responsible for these formations? All three ciphers *must* be the result of applied intelligence. Nobody will dispute this, not even the supporters of the 'plasma-vortex' theory, nor the sceptics who regard all crop circles as a product of human hoaxers. Indeed, if some or all of these three ciphers were human work, it raises a lot of questions, not least about the motive.

What purpose would humans have in mind? Could they be part of a group which aims to increase the psychological impact of a natural phenomenon which they regard as important? Does somebody, as some suspect, intend to create a cult? Or are they just remarkably educated and knowledgeable hoaxers who have no other motive than playing games with the expectations of people who are fascinated by the mysterious marks in the crop, and the ambiguity of the phenomenon they are dealing with? Crop circles have a material, conspiratorial and even a dark aspect, and at the same time an undeniably spiritual and metaphysical side.

Let us look at the various explanations which are on offer. A non-human intelligence, beings from other worlds and dimensions, time-travellers from the future, a cosmic consciousness perhaps — or are the circles a message from parallel worlds? Others believe in some form of resonance in the collective human consciousness, applying the idea of Rupert Sheldrake's *morphogenetic fields*.[2] Others, again, tend to think of the circles as some form of communication between Gaia (the living, global, self-regulating super-organism advocated by James Lovelock[3]) and the human species, in order to warn humankind not to pursue its destructive treatment of the earth.

Another interesting suggestion comes from the astrophysicist and UFO researcher Jacques Vallée[4]. He thinks it is possible, and in this opinion he is not alone, that the circles are a result of testing of a space-based 'Star Wars' technology. Vallée talks about microwave beam weapons whose precision might be tested using corn-stems as some kind of microwave antenna to create accurate formations in the fields. Vallée suggests that such a classified experiment would at the same time be a physical and sociological exercise, using new-age beliefs and extraterrestrial expectations as a cover. If this cover were in danger of being lifted, there would always be the chance to fall back on the ground-based hoax theory, so vividly represented by Doug and Dave.

In the present state of affairs it is impossible to be sure which explanation is right, whatever personal preferences one might have. No hypothesis or theory covers all aspects of this strange and exciting phenomenon. What we can do at the moment, however, is refute the idea that all circles and formations are merely the result of humans running around in the fields. We definitely do need more scientific data — every faction in crop circle research and beliefs agree with that. It is the only way to establish this phenomenon in its own right, although we should not *over*-estimate the benefit of scientific evidence. It is quite likely that the 'citadel of science', and the media, may choose to ignore uncomfortable facts, as they have done before. The hitherto-available results of laboratory research into soil and crop samples already lay to rest the idea of a ground-based hoax. The results are preliminary, but interesting enough: significant changes in radiation levels, changes in the cell-structure of the growth-nodes, carbon-blackening and 'polyembronio', a very uncommon genetic aberration which leads to legumes without any seeds.[4]

In this context one should not forget the growing interest of Japanese scientists. From year to year they have spent more time and money for research of the crop circle phenomenon. Professor Yoshi Hiko Ohtsuki has already patented the circle-forming plasma. It is possible that, coming from a country which is poorly endowed with fossil fuels, they may be looking for a new cheap form of energy. It shows how the Japanese scientists are not dominated by the fear of an 'unknown anomaly' as are so many of their European and American colleagues.

Where do we go from here? I think, with what we know so far, *it is important and necessary to avoid a decision in favour of but one explanation*. Our perception is still uncertain — therefore it is impossible to derive certain conclusions from uncertain perceptions. The phenomenon may be even more complex than we can imagine. As Robert Anton Wilson recommended, *never accept one belief-system completely, especially not your most favourite one*.

What we can be certain of is the effect of the circles on human consciousness. It is therefore worthwhile and necessary to look at the way in which the phenomenon impresses itself on the human mind. Nobody can deny that the circles have changed the perception of many people — they have even significantly changed the lives of quite a few! People like Colin Andrews and George Wingfield have given up good jobs in order to study the phenomenon. Beth Davis and Brian Grist, as well as so many others, give much of their spare time to research and writing. Someone like Pat Delgado, a veteran of crop circle research, dedicates his retirement to writing books and healing. Whatever all these researchers and crop circle experts do, whichever path they choose, there is a common pattern evolving: the rejection of the old mechanistic and materialistic world-view.

Some, like Colin Andrews, preach the message of 'Mother Earth crying out'. In so doing, they support the idea of a 'living earth' — a worthy task, because if only we grasp this idea, if we understand, that we are *part of* nature, we may stop behaving as if we were its cruel master, as both Bacon and Marx propagated. Many dowsers, such as Richard Andrews, David Tilt and Hamish Miller, have discovered a connection between circles and the subtle energy-grid, or if you prefer, the acupuncture lines and points of the earth. They help to revive the knowledge of the more subtle forces of nature, a knowledge which industrial civilisation has forgotten or ignored at its own peril.

The interpretation of crop-symbolism of Michael Green and others, however controversial they may be, fulfil an important function as well: they help to widen our view, to remind us that the history of humankind has not been an uninterrupted, smooth process, with humanity marching ahead to new heights of progress. The history of humankind and the history of nature are not to be separated, for they are inextricably linked. Both have been interrupted by cataclysms, dark ages and the loss of knowledge — they can regress as well as progress.

In this scenario, Terence Meaden, with his plasma-vortex theory, plays a part too. His theory underlines the fact that our knowledge of nature is incomplete, that there are anomalies which science hasn't recognised. The plasma-vortex theory is also a challenge to orthodox science. No wonder that Meaden is regarded as an outsider by the scientific community. This may explain why he is so obviously torn between two different feelings: he is irresistibly attracted to the crop circle phenomenon, driven into the territory of prehistory (in so doing, irritating archaeologists), writing about the mystical impact and the religion-creating function of his vortex[5]. Meaden even overcame the 'immunological reflex' of the scientific community, and accepted the reality of the UFO-phenomenon, which, as he proposes, can be explained by his plasma-vortex theory as well. At the same time he is extremely wary of losing his scientific credibility, distancing himself sharply and, as some complain, arrogantly from all other researchers, and pursuing his research ever more secretively.

Many people and groups have been drawn to the crop circle phenomenon. Some, as in the case of John MacNish, have set up film companies with telling names like 'CircleVision'. Others photograph and video the circles (Busty Taylor), or measure and draw the pictograms in the crops. And then there is John Michell, following discussions and developments with gentle irony and mild humour, having seen it all before — he wrote and talked about the challenge of earth mysteries, anomalies and the evolution of a new worldview long before crop circles had attracted our attention, or had appeared in the fields of Britain. "No society which is based on entirely rational or single-minded principles can endure for any great length of time. Any philosophy which advocates the continued rape of this earth is inimical to human interests because it threatens the very existence of our living earth." And he added that the political consequences of the now-dominant cosmology "may prove quite as menacing as its physical effects". At the same time, with his magazine *The Cerealogist*, he presents an urgently-needed forum for discussion and exchange of opinions.

No doubt: the crop circle phenomenon has accelerated an already-existing process of change in belief-systems. You only have to go out into the cornfields, speak to people, listen to their opinions and feelings, and you will find out what a dramatic change is taking place, a change in world-view, a paradigm change. The crop circle phenomenon is only one of many subversive anomalies that trigger change and spark off a new way of thinking. The new belief-system which is evolving embraces the paranormal, the parascientific, the spiritual and the extraterrestrial while not denying science and technology. It is 'Gaia-centred', and touches on green ideas, especially 'deep ecology'. Part of the new world-view is the search for the mystic roots of religions, of Christianity, Judaism and Islam, such as Gnosticism, Kabbalah and Sufism.

The dominating religion of world civilisation, science, is in a process of disillusion. Its uneasy ally of the last 300 years since the 'Age of Enlightenment', Christianity, is also in a crisis, as leading churchmen quite frankly admit. Its critics accuse Christianity of complicity with materialism, for having abandoned its spiritual and metaphysical message. Science based on Newton, Kepler and Descartes (though Newton and Kepler had their doubts and pursued studies on other, more metaphysical levels) was once energetic and influential. Modern physics and mathematics were the pillars of this new materialistic religion. Doubts about the mechanistic world-view have grown significantly stronger in the last two decades: more and more people are convinced that it was this secular religion which has led humankind into a destructive dead end.

It is worth remembering what Egon Friedell wrote, more than 60 years ago in his '*Geschichte der Neuzeit*' (*History of Modern Times*): "What I try to describe is the short interlude of the rule of rationalism between two 'irrationalisms', the medieval one and the one of the future. This interlude represents no more than an elusive fashion, an interesting eccentricity, a cultural curiosity." Egon Friedell, Arnold Toynbee and others were never convinced that the rule of the intellect could really be called 'rational. Toynbee warned that we had become 'technological giants' but remained 'moral pygmies'.

The most important question facing humankind is whether or not it will be able to close the gap between the global consequences of its actions and the individual- or group-oriented ethos. Today we are better equipped to understand why doing this is essential. The main assumption of the dominating world-view of the last three hundred years is clearly wrong. More material goods and ever higher standards of consumption have not led to a higher quality of life. On the contrary. The spread of material wealth in western societies did not prevent them from becoming more violent; crime is spreading, the signs of disintegration are becoming visible everywhere. The global crisis is deepening every day. The political, social and economic consequences which result from the greenhouse effect, ozone depletion and dramatically shrinking resources of an over-populated and abused planet will be severe, and will affect all nations.

Science had claimed to solve the problems of the world and bring happiness to humanity. Even the most hardened and optimistic supporters of the doctrine of materialism and progress don't dare to seriously advocate this belief any longer. We have reached a crisis in our relationship with the earth. The excesses of materialism are clearly visible, and its consequences can't be denied any longer. The hasty and nevertheless unsatisfactory decisions by our governments in the face of growing global crisis are an admission. The number of global conferences has increased dramatically. This represents a hopeful development — however, slowly global awareness is beginning to grow. It is no contradiction that one nevertheless can see their outcomes as a failure and an expression of helplessness: whatever decisions have been made at world climate summits or international ozone-layer conferences, they won't stand the judgement of time for more than a short period — not even in the eyes of the political and business classes.

A telling example was the panicky reaction of multinationals and western governments, among them Washington, Bonn and London, to speed up the ending of CFC production, after scientists had discovered significant depletion of ozone over the northern hemisphere, in our own backyard. We can be sure that more and more drastic decisions will be taken in the near future: the emission of climate-altering greenhouse gases will have to be reduced more drastically, and the production of CFCs will need to be phased out even earlier than what was suggested by the last round of decisions. But the race against time will be lost if it not accompanied by a deeper understanding of the causes of the present global dilemma.

Many people are convinced that the planet, and with it humanity, can't survive as long as the old materialistic paradigm rules. They believe that the earth and humankind cannot be saved by reason and technology alone. What is needed is to replace the economic growth and affluence obsession, to give up the greed principle, all of which are the underlying causes of global destruction.

The emergent world-view tries to end the spiritual void of modern civilisation. It promotes a shift to a post-modern and at the same time ancient reverence for nature. It develops a holistic view of life and the universe. This could be called 'eco-faith' or 'Gaia spirituality'; it has triggered, in the words of Fritjof Capra, a shift of values "from self-assertion and competition to cooperation and social justice, from expansion to conservation, from material acquisition to inner growth".

The crop circle community, in spite of its faults and weaknesses, its rivalry and jealousy is part of the wider process towards a new paradigm. Will this post-materialistic and spiritual tendency in our western societies develop into a full-blown religion, as some critical observers fear? If the answer is yes, then there still would be significant differences to what we regard as established religions. The new belief-system is varied and unstructured, it has no church, no dogma, it doesn't know centralised authority, but it shares ethic, myth, values and not least symbols, and is open-minded and easy-going enough to consider ciphers in the crops as signs of some importance.

The new world-view draws from a wide range of ideas and sources: alchemy, paganism, oriental and western mysticism, Jungian psychology, ecology, alternative medicine and earth mysteries. Insights of the new sciences encourage the followers of the new model: they see that 'science and magic meet'; they believe that more and more scientific breakthroughs support the truth of old pre-materialistic religions. Indeed, the Gaia Theory has brought together life-sciences and geophysical sciences. Rupert Sheldrake proposes a field theory which combines an animated nature, the universe and God.

Physics, once the pillar on which mechanistic reductionism was built, is now at the forefront of a transformation. Many scientists now see the world very differently. The idea of the universe as a clockwork, gigantic machine without purpose is being laid to rest — the 'matter myth' has been destroyed by quantum physics. The collapse of communism, with its materialist dogma, is so far the strongest indication of the global decline of the materialistic paradigm.

The impact of the spiritual revolution infiltrating the industrial societies can be detected even in government. Education secretary John Patten, suggested the main reason for the spiral of crime and violence is the "dwindling belief in redemption and damnation". It is interesting that a leading politician sees 'lack of faith' as the main reason why things go wrong in modern societies.

Leader article writers lament the effects of secularisation, and state that "ours is the civilisation of instant gratification" (*Daily Telegraph*), while at the same time endorsing political parties and governments unreservedly married to the idea of growth and consumerism. A thoughtful establishment figure like Sir William Rees-Mogg criticises the 'telebabble' of the 1992 election campaign, and notices a 'metanoia' below the surface of traditional politics, a change of consciousness in the western world, a rejection of the 'slavery' of addiction to things. "That is why meditation is gaining adherents, why many of the most intelligent do not wish to clutter themselves with worldly goods, and why many of the best students do not seek to maximise their incomes." Rees-Mogg's latest book with the telling title '*The Great Reckoning*' frightens its readers with dark visions of global unrest and breakdown. He recommends a particular mix of guidelines like "get committed", "stop shopping", "turn off the television", which all have a clearly-recognisable touch of new age, and financial advice for making money in hard times.[6]

But not all representatives and institutions of the established world look at the evolving post-materialistic consciousness with the same understanding, or even mild sympathy. 'New Age beliefs' are attacked by members of the Church of England as 'devil worship', as in the case of the Reverend Tony Higton, one of the Church's more militant neo-fundamentalists. Some professing Christians regard crop circles as 'evil', in the same context as alleged ritual child-abuse and satanic rites, a myth created first in America, and now in Britain, by Christian fundamentalists.

In a pamphlet for the Institute of European Defence and Strategic Studies, Andrew McHallam argues on a more sophisticated level. He finds that the new movement "has many of the characteristics of a new religion. It offers both an apocalyptic vision of the future, and a means of redemption if mankind repents". McHallam foresees the rise of 'new authoritarians', a religious 'eco-fascism', and predicts the

threat of a 'new inquisition', emerging as a by-product of the new
religion.

Accusations such as this underline the fact that times of paradigm
shift are times of intense conflict. The battle-lines are drawn for a new
religious war, according to Walter Schwarz of the *Guardian*. The
representatives of the old mechanistic order will not give up without a
fight. The resistance will become stronger the more they feel their
position to be under threat. The attacks on 'dangerous irrationalism'
will increase, and will be targeted against groups which promote the
new model and alternative scientific ideas.

It is no coincidence that a neo-Darwinist like Richard Dawkins,
wedded to the mechanism of inheritance and natural selection, takes
on Lovelock's Gaia Theory, one of the fundaments of the new world
view: "the Gaia Theory thrives on an innate desire, mostly among
lay-people, to believe that evolution works for the good of all.
Profoundly erroneous!" Perhaps this attack was provoked by James
Lovelock's remark that Gaia "may turn out to be the first religion to
have a testable scientific theory buried in it".

The 'dissidents of the Nineties', the 'Gaians', the dowsers and
channellers, should be aware of the danger that the longing of many
people for a spiritual world-view can be perverted or abused by
charlatans and power-seeking prophets, who claim to possess *the*
truth. They should remember that they are still a minority, albeit
growing. Their enthusiasm, their readiness to accept that there is a
thrust forward to higher consciousness, that they witness the 'shama-
nising of modern humanity', will be met with scepticism and ridicule,
if not suspicion and hostility. The events around the crop circles have
provided enough examples!

NOTES

1. Michell, John, *The Cerealogist*, no. 4 (Summer 1991).
2. Sheldrake, Rupert, *The Rebirth of Nature*, Century, 1990.
3. Lovelock, James, *Gaia, A New Look at Life on Earth*, Oxford Univ Press, 1979.
4. Keen, Montagu, *1991 – Scientific Evidence for the Crop Circle Phenomenon*, Elvery Dowers Pubs, for the CCCS.
5. Meaden, Terence, *The Goddess of the Stones*, Souvenir, 1991.
6. Rees-Mogg, Sir William, *The Great Reckoning*, Sidgwick & Jackson, 1991.

Further Reading

Books on Crop Circles

Bartholomew, Alick, ed. *Crop Circles – Harbingers of World Change*, Gateway Books, Bath, 1991.

Delgado, Pat, and Andrews, Colin, *Circular Evidence*, Bloomsbury, London, 1989.

Delgado, Pat, and Andrews, Colin, *Latest Evidence*, Bloomsbury, London, 1990.

Jung, Carl, *Flying Saucers: A Modern Myth of Things Seen in the Skies*, Routledge & Kegan Paul, London, 1959.

Keen, Montague, *Scientific Evidence for the Crop Circle Phenomena*, Elvery Dowes, Norwich, 1992.

Krönig, Jürgen, *Spuren im Korn, Zweitausendeins*, Frankfurt, 1992 (in German).

Meaden, Terence, *The Circles Effect and its Mysteries*, Artetech, Bradford-on-Avon, 1989.

Michell, John, *Dowsing the Crop Circles*, Gothic Image, Glastonbury, 1991.

Noyes, Ralph, ed. *Crop Circle Enigma*, Gateway, Bath, 1990.

Noyes, Ralph, *Crop Circles – is there a Paranormal Factor?*, The Psi Researcher, July 1991, Society for Psychical Research.

Palgrave-Moore, Patrick, *Crop Circle Classification*, Elvery Dowes, Norwich, 1991.

Wingfield, George, "The English Corn Circles in 1988", *The UFO Report*, 1990, edited by Timothy Good, Sidgwick & Jackson, London, 1989.

Books on related subjects

Alexandersson, Olof, *Living Water: Viktor Schauberger and the Secrets of Natural Energy*, Gateway, Bath, 1990.

Arguelles, Jose, *The Mayan Factor*, Bear & Co, 1985. *Black Dawn, Bright Day*, Sun Bear, Sun Press.

Ash, David, and Hewitt, Peter, *Science of the Gods, Reconciling Mystery and Matter*, Gateway Books, Bath, 1991.

Attenborough, David, *Life on Earth*, Collins, London, 1979.

Barrett, F, *The Magus*, London, 1801. Reprinted Aquarian Press, London, 1989.

Barrow, John, *The World Within the World*, Oxford Univ Press, 1988.

Briggs, J, & Peat, F D, *Turbulent Mirror: An Illustrated Guide to Chaos Theory and the Science of Wholeness*, Harper & Row, New York, 1989.

Bronowski, Jacob, *The Ascent of Man*, BBC Publications, London, 1973.

Butler, W E, *Lords of Light*, Destiny Books, New York, 1990.

Cooper, J C, *An Illustrated Encyclopaedia of Traditional Symbols*, Thames & Hudson, London, 1978.

Davies, Paul, *Superforce – The Search for a Grand Unified Theory of Nature*, Unwin, London, 1985.

de Givry, Grillot, *Witchcraft, Magic & Alchemy*, London, 1931. Reprinted Dover, New York, 1971.

de Rola, Stanislas Klossowski, *Alchemy: the Secret Art*, Thames & Hudson, London, 1973.

Devereux, Paul, *Earth Memory*, Quantum, London, 1991.

Fabricius, Johannes, *Alchemy*, Copenhagen, 1976. Reprinted Aquarian Press, London, 1989.

von Franz, Marie-Louise, *Alchemy: an Introduction to the Symbolism and the Psychology*, Inner City Books, Toronto, 1980.

Gilchrist, Cherry, *Alchemy*, Element Books, Shaftesbury, 1991.

Gleick, James, *Chaos: Making a New Science*, Heinemann, London, 1988. Reprinted Cardinal, 1988.

Halevi, Z'ev ben Shimon, *The Tree of Life: an Introduction to the Kabbalah*, London, 1972. Reprinted Gateway Books, Bath, 1991.

Hall, Nina, ed, *The New Scientist Guide to Chaos*, Penguin, London, 1991.

Joseph, L E, *Gaia, the Growth of an Idea*, Arkana, 1991.

Jung, C G, *Psychology & Alchemy*, Routledge & Kegan Paul, London, 1953.

Jung, C G, *The Undiscovered Self*, Routledge & Kegan Paul, London, 1958.

Jung, C G, *Alchemical Studies*, Routledge & Kegan Paul, London, 1967.

Lonegren, Sig, *Labyrinths, their Construction and Uses*, Gothic Image, Glastonbury, 1989.

Lonegren, Sig, *Spiritual Dowsing*, Gothic Image, Glastonbury, 1987.

Lovelock, J E, *Gaia: A New Look at Life on Earth*, Oxford Univ Press, 1979.

Men, Hunbatz, *Secrets of Mayan Science and Religion*, Bear & Co, 1990.

Purse, Jill, *The Mystic Spiral*, Thames & Hudson, London, 1974.

Michelspacher, Steffan, *Cabala, Speculum Artis et Naturae, in Alchymia*, Augsburg, 1654.

Russell, Peter, *The Awakening Earth — Our Next Evolutionary Leap*, Routledge & Kegan Paul, London, 1982.

Sheldrake, Rupert, *The Presence of the Past*, Collins, London, 1988.

Sheldrake, Rupert, *The Rebirth of Nature*, Random Century, London, 1990.

Schneider, Stephen, *Global Warming*, Lutterworth, Cambridge, 1989.

Stewart, Ian, *Does God Play Dice? The New Mathematics of Chaos*, Blackwell, London, 1989.

Teilhard de Chardin, Pierre, *The Phenomenon of Man*, Collins, London, 1959.

Thunderhorse/Donnlevie, Iron, *Return of the Thunderbeings*, Bear & Co, 1990.

Wade, David, *Crystal and Dragon: the Cosmic Two-Step*, Resurgence, Bideford, 1992.

Waite, A E, ed, *The Hermetic Museum*, London, 1893. Reprinted Weiser, Maine, 1990.

Videos

Baum, Miriam, *The Mandelbrot Set*, Glastonbury 1991.

MacNish, John, *Crop Circle Communique*, Circlevision, 1991.

Matrix, Art, *Mandelbrot Sets and Julia Sets*, Hubbard Dynamical Systems Laboratory Film, New York, 1990.

Contributors

Beth Davis is a conservation officer dealing with historic buildings in Cambridgeshire. She lectures on building history and landscape history. She also uses her dowsing skills to identify and interpret ancient sites with groups of her students. She is a founder member of the Centre for Crop Circle Studies.

Brian Grist was brought up in Warminster, a Wiltshire town familiar with mysteries. He has a special interest in the relationship of geology and underground water to crop circles and first became interested in the phenomenon in 1983. He is a history and literature graduate from Bath College of Higher Education, and works as a bookseller in Bristol.

Gary Hardwick shares many field research interests with Brian Grist, and is particularly fascinated by archeology and prehistory. A graduate in law from N.E.London Polytechnic, he now works in life assurance in Bristol.

Jürgen Krönig is the political editor and British correspondent for ARD Radio Centre and the newspaper Die Zeit. An inveterate crop-watcher, he has edited *Spuren im Korn*; a very comprehensive recent German book on the crop circle phenomena. He lives on the Marlborough Downs.

John Wakefield's interest in shamanism was kindled by Carlos Castenda's books in the 1970's. **Julie Wakefield**'s lifelong interest in North American Indian traditions brought them together. John has a deep interest in mycology, and Julie in homoeopathy. They have been studying crop circles for three years, and live in Manchester.

George Wingfield was educated at Eton College and Trinity College, Dublin, in natural sciences. He worked at the Royal Greenwich Observatory, Herstmonceux, on stellar spectra and terrestrial magnetism, and for many years with IBM in systems engineering. He is a founder member of the Centre for Crop Circle Studies, and his interests include paraphysics and ufology.

Index